CHURCH AT THE END OF THE 20TH

DATE DUE

RIVERSIDE CITY COLLEGE
LIBRARY

Riverside, California

1975

DEMCO—FRESNO

other books by Francis A. Schaeffer

Escape from Reason
The God Who Is There
Death in the City
Pollution and the Death of Man
The Mark of the Christian

THE CHURCH AT THE END OF THE 20TH CENTURY BY FRANCIS A. SCHAEFFER

Inter-Varsity Press
Downers Grove
Illinois 60515

Material from the International
Herald Tribune *is reprinted (on page 98) by
permission of The Associated Press.*

© *1970 by Francis A. Schaeffer*

Third printing, March 1972

*Inter-Varsity Press
is the book publishing division
of Inter-Varsity Christian Fellowship.*

ISBN 0-87784-889-0
Library of Congress Catalog Card Number: 73-134795

Printed in the United States of America

contents

preface

In this book, I have attempted to describe the sociological milieu in which the church of Jesus Christ now finds itself. Amidst an international student revolution, and in the midst of a culture cut loose not only from God and revelation, but also cut loose from reason—in a society easily subject to manipulation by a New Left or an Establishment elite—what future is there for the institutional church? It is in the context of this question that the present book has been written.

Those who have read my previous books, especially *The God Who Is There* and *Escape from Reason,* will find some repetition in chapter one of this present book. However, three things should be kept in mind: (1) For those who have not read the other books, this base—"how we got to be where we are"—must be laid, or the rest of the book floats in space. (2) Some new material is added which will be helpful in viewing the total context in its specific sociological perspective. (3) Even for those who have read the other books a number of times, listened to my taped lectures or heard me lecture in person, a review will still not be amiss, for the material in chapter one should be consciously before all of us as we consider "where we are" in regard to the church in the midst of the present and future sociological situation.

Furthermore, this analysis emphasizes and reemphasizes the fact that modern problems in many fields are really not many, but one basic problem with a number of results in what at first may seem to be unrelated fields or disciplines. Thus, the modern cultural problem, the sociological problem, the problem of governing our countries today, the problems of ecology and epistemology are all related, for the basic problem of modern man gives the specific form with which each of these confronts us. And if our comprehension of this relatedness is not clear at its base, we cannot give basic solutions to effect a cure.

On the other hand, I would urge those who have not read the other books and who feel chapter one moves too quickly to read the book-length treatments in *The God Who Is There* and *Escape from Reason.*

Francis A. Schaeffer
L'Abri Fellowship
Switzerland

1

the roots of the student revolution

Everywhere men are asking if the church has a future as we come to the close of the 20th century. To consider this we must first think through where we are and what we can expect as we approach the end of this century. Let us first consider the international student revolution and its relationship to society as a whole and let us begin this by tracing quickly how in our society we got to be where we are.

The international student revolution did not spontaneously appear from nowhere. Its true and deepest roots are seen in the stream of intellectual history which flows from the European Renaissance and before. It is a revolution that is not merely cultural or psychological. Its source is not to be found in a simplistic analysis of the generation gap. The roots strike deep into the history of man and his attempt to understand who he is and where he came from.

It is just such intellectual history that we must grasp if we are to comprehend the ferment on our campuses today.

the rise of science

The birth of modern science is the place to begin. Modern science arose out of a Christian mentality. Alfred North Whitehead, for example, emphasizes the fact that modern science was born because it was surrounded by a Christian frame of reference. Galileo, Copernicus, Francis Bacon, Kepler and scientists up to and including Newton believed that the world was created by a reasonable God and therefore we could find out the order of the universe by reason.

Oppenheimer stressed the same thing: Modern science could not have been born at all without a Christian milieu, a Christian consensus. As Francis Bacon (1561-1626) said in *Novum Organum Scientiarum:* "Man by the Fall fell at the same time from his state of innocence and from his dominion over nature. Both of these losses, however, can even in this life be in some part repaired; the former by religion and faith, the latter by the arts and the sciences." Recently I read something from Galileo which was very moving to me. Galileo stressed the fact that, when he looked at the universe in all its richness and its beauty (he did not mean merely aesthetic beauty but its unity in the midst of its complexity), he was called to only one end—to worship the beauty of the Creator.

This was the birth of our modern thinking in the area of science and it produced various results. It led, for example, to the certainty of the uniformity of natural causes. There was a uniformity of natural causes, not in the closed system, but in one that was open to reordering.

Early modern scientists believed that God and man could operate into the machine and reorder the flow of cause and effect.

This had a number of results. First, it meant that nature was important. Second, it implied a clear distinction between nature as the object and myself as the observer. There was an objective basis for knowledge—something out there—and there was, therefore, a clear distinction between reality and fantasy. The people who gave birth to modern science knew that God had created the universe, that it was there, not as Eastern thinking has it, as an extension of the essence of God, but as something other than God and as something other than what is spun out of the mind of man. Today this objective basis for knowledge has been undermined and the distinction between reality and fantasy has become difficult—sometimes impossible—to maintain.[1]

Furthermore, as is obvious from the quotation above, Bacon believed that man was wonderful, even though he was fallen. He believed in the fall of man in the biblical sense—that man is a sinner shut away from God on the basis of his moral guilt. Nevertheless, man is wonderful.

This is the very opposite of modern man. Modern man has been told that reason has led to the conclusion that man is a zero. This is a part of the tension of our present generation. It did not exist when modern science began. In those days, in other words, the machine was no threat, neither the machine of the cosmos nor the machines that man made.

the particular and the universal

The Greeks long before understood that there was a dilemma between the particulars and the universals. It was not only Plato who wrestled with this, but he understood exactly what Jean-Paul Sartre has said in our generation: A finite point has no meaning unless it has an infinite reference point. He is right. Unless the particulars have a universal over them, the particulars have no meaning. Whether a particular is an atom, or a chair, or you, there must be a relationship to something which gives it meaning, or these things all become zero.

The Greeks sought answers to the dilemma in two different realms. First of all, in the area of the *polis*. The Greek concept of *polis* involves far

---

[1] The problem of epistemology is central to the problem of modern man and I have discussed it in much more detail in a book entitled *He Is There and He Is Not Silent*, to be published by Tyndale House Publishers in the United States and by Hodder and Stoughton in Britain.

more than just a city—though that is the literal definition of the word. It implies a whole society. And the Greeks found that society as society could not give ample meaning to the particulars.

Second, they tried to place the particulars in relation to their gods. But the difficulty with the Greek gods is that they never were big enough to be an infinite reference point. Greek literature shows this in the way the Fates are treated. Sometimes the Fates are in control and sometimes the gods control the Fates. Thus, neither society nor their gods gave them a sufficient universal.

Moving very rapidly to another crucial point in history, the high Renaissance, one encounters Leonardo da Vinci, the first modern mathematician. Leonardo tried to find an infinite reference point from the standpoint of rationalism or humanism—terms which I am using as synonyms, though one could use them otherwise. What rationalism or humanism is must be made clear here, because it is so easily confused with the word rational. Rationalism means that man begins from himself and tries to build all the answers on this base, receiving nothing from any other source and specifically refusing any revelation from God. Such rejection of revelation has led in our era to the position of the early Wittgenstein and the movie *The Silence* by the modern film maker, Ingmar Bergman. There is no one there to speak. Leonardo felt this silence in regard to a rationalistic universal back in his day.

Leonardo first tried to find an infinite reference point by means of mathematics. But he realized as a mathematician that if you begin with mathematics, you only get to particulars and to mechanics. You do not discover or produce a universal.[2]

Recognizing that mathematics could not give him the proper base, Leonardo then tried to see if the artist could paint the soul. By *soul*, he did not mean the same thing as a theologian does. Rather he meant the universal. He totally failed.

The fact is that man, beginning with only particulars, can never derive the universal. And that is as true in metaphysics as in morals.

rousseau and autonomous freedom

Next, in order to understand the student revolution today, one must properly understand Jean Jacques Rousseau. The Durants in their history of

---

[2] See Giovanni Gentile, *Leonardo da Vinci* (New York: Raynal and Company, 1956), p. 174.

mankind begin their study of modern man quite properly with Rousseau. They rightly say that you cannot understand modern man without understanding him. Back in the time of the high Renaissance, the intellectuals wrestled with the problem of nature and grace, a subject dealt with especially in *Escape from Reason*. Jean Jacques Rousseau was concerned with nature and freedom. This is the background of student freedom—the autonomous freedom which modern man seeks. Rousseau saw that by his time rationalistic man had reduced the created world (nature) to an autonomous machine. By the time of Rousseau men were already feeling threatened by the machine and so they set up autonomous freedom against the machine. Reasonably you cannot have both an autonomous machine, a machine that encompasses everything including man, and autonomous freedom at the same time. Nevertheless, Rousseau put forth the concept. Here Kant follows in the same direction, but uses different terminology.

The lines of opposition are clear: On the one hand is a determinism—an autonomous machine; on the other hand is a man who desires autonomous freedom to stand against the restriction of the machine and all restrictions. What began to develop was a Bohemian life. In this situation the artist living the Bohemian life became the hero. In the autonomous life, not only were the constraints of Scripture being cast away, but all restraints. Civilization began, therefore, to be seen as the threatening force, the demonic force, which limited the individual's freedom. The Bohemian life never worked out well in practice.

Rousseau himself wrote on how to raise children. But his theories failed to work even for himself. Most people do not realize that he had children whom he put in an institution and never or rarely visited. Here is the problem of the autonomous freedom: It leads to the selfish and the ugly.

Gauguin the artist did exactly the same thing. He went off to Tahiti to find his ideal away from culture and away from society, but all the time he was away, his family back in Paris was writing to him, asking for money for the food they lacked. But the concept of autonomous freedom led him not to care. He left an illegitimate son in Tahiti—about the only contribution he made there. He left a child who had to snatch small amounts of money from the tourists through the years by painting horrible paintings and signing them Gauguin. Not very pretty—the result of the concept of the autonomous freedom, the Bohemian life.

Gauguin himself at the end of his life recognized that this autonomous freedom was not going to work, and he shows this in his great painting, *What? Whence? Whither?* which hangs now in the Boston Museum of Art.

It took him two years to do this painting, and the French inscription painted on the canvas itself tells us what he was doing. In other words, he asks, "Where are we going?" In his letters he called attention to the last three figures, a very beautiful Tahitian girl, an old woman, and an ugly bird, of which there is no counterpart in nature. He makes plain in his writings what he is saying in this painting: Notice the last three figures. Notice the old woman—she is dying, and who is watching her? Nobody but a bird that doesn't exist. There is the dilemma. Autonomous freedom did not work out even in Gauguin's own lifetime.

modern science and modern, modern science

Later we come to the difference between modern science and what I call modern, modern science. Modern science was born, as I have indicated, from the Christian concept that man on the basis of reason could understand the universe because a God of reason had created it. Modern, modern science, however, extended the idea of the uniformity of natural causes by adding a new phrase—*in a closed system.* This little phrase changed all of life because it put everything within the machine.

At first science dealt with physics, chemistry and astronomy. You could add a few more subjects, perhaps, but there it ended. But later as psychology was added and then social sciences, man himself was in the machine.

If everything is put into the machine, of course, there is no place for God. But also there is no place for man, no place for the significance of man, no place for beauty, for morals or for love. When you come to this place, you have a sea without a shore. Everything is dead. But the presupposition of the uniformity of natural causes in a closed system does not explain the two basic things that stand before us: (1) the universe that exists and its form and (2) the mannishness of man.

As Sartre says, the basic philosophic question is that something is there rather than not being there. You have to explain that something that is there. Einstein adds a note: When we examine the universe, we find that it is like a well-formulated word puzzle; namely, that you can suggest any word, but finally only one will fit. In other words you not only have a universe that is there that has to be explained, but it is a very special kind of a universe, a very "nice" universe as far as complexity and order are concerned.

Modern man in his philosophy, his music and his art usually depicts a chaotic situation in the universe. But when you make a Boeing 707, it is beautiful. Why? Because it fits into the universe. The universe is not really the chaos that they picture.

There is also the problem of the mannishness of man. Over 60,000 years ago—if you accept modern dating—man buried his dead in flower petals. If we look at Chinese bronzes, though they are far separated from us in time and culture, we find they conform to ourselves. They were made by somebody else, but they are also a part of me. There is the mannishness of man. The cave paintings at 20,000-30,000 B.C. are even more illustrative. From these one can show that man has always felt himself to be different from non-man.

Modern man says, "No, we are just machines—chemically determined or psychologically determined." But nobody consistently lives this way in his life. I would insist that here is a presupposition which intellectually, in the laboratory, would be cast out simply because it does not explain what is.

On the other hand, the biblical position which begins with a personal rather than an impersonal beginning gives us another answer. The real issue is to decide, with intellectual integrity, which set of presuppositions really conforms to what is.

But many of us catch our presuppositions like measles. Why do people fit into the post-Christian world? I would urge that it is not because of facts, but because our present almost monolithic culture has forced upon us the other answer—namely, the uniformity of natural causes, not in an open system beginning with a personal God, the way the early scientists believed, but in a closed system. It is not that the facts are against the Christian presuppositions, but simply that the Christian view is presented as unthinkable. The better the university, the better the brainwashing.

The results of following the implications of modern man were clearly developed in the 19th century. Nobody has expressed it better than the Marquis de Sade, who was one of the early modern chemical determinists. De Sade's position (and he lived by it) was that if you have determinism then whatever *is* is right. You can say that things are non-social. Or you can think of Tillich's concept of the demonic as being a force for disintegration rather than for integration, but that is all you can say. You cannot say that anything is right or wrong. Morality is dead. Man is dead.

Nietzsche is the key to this. He was the first man who cried, in the modern sense, "God is dead," but he was brilliant enough to understand the results. If God is dead, then everything is gone. I believe that it was not just his venereal disease in Switzerland which caused him to become insane. I believe that Nietzsche made a philosophic statement in his insanity.

He understood that if God is dead, there are no answers to anything and insanity is the end. This is not too far philosophically from the modern Michael Foucault, for example, who says that the only freedom is in insanity.

What one is left with in such a situation we must never forget. If we do not begin with a personal Creator, eventually we are left (no matter how we string it out semantically) with the impersonal plus time plus chance. We must explain everything in the mannishness of man and we must understand all of the complexity of the universe on the basis of time plus chance.

The difficulty of explaining man and the universe on such a basis was recognized by Darwin himself. In his autobiography and in letters published by his son he wrote: With my mind I cannot believe that these things come by chance. He said this as an old man many times over. Twice he added a strange note to this effect: "I know in my mind this can't be true, but my mind is only a monkey's mind, and who can trust a mind like that?" But, of course, this raises a problem. On this basis, how could one accept any conclusions of the human mind, including Darwin's theory?

More recently, Murray Eden at MIT has been using high-speed computers to ask a question: Beginning with chaos at any acceptable amount of time up to eight billion years ago, could the present complexity come by chance? So far the answer is absolutely *No*.

cosmic alienation

But modern man does in fact assume—wittingly or unwittingly—that the universe and man can be explained by the impersonal plus time plus chance. And in this case man and his aspirations stand in total alienation from what is. And that is precisely where students today live—in a generation of alienation. Alienation in the ghettos, alienation in the university, alienation from parents, alienation on every side. Sometimes those who are only playing with these ideas and have not gotten down into the real guts of it forget that the basic alienation with which they are faced is a cosmic alienation. Simply this: There is nobody there to respond to you. There is nobody home in the universe. There is no one and nothing there to conform to who you are or what you hope. That is the dilemma.

Let me use an illustration I have used previously. Suppose, for example, that the room in which you are seated is the only universe there is. God could have made a universe just this big if he wished. Suppose in making the only universe there were a room made up of solid walls, but filled up to the ceiling with liquids: just liquids and solids and no free gases. Suppose then that fish were swimming in the universe. The fish would not be alienated from the universe because they can conform to the universe by their nature. But suppose if by chance, as the evolutionists see chance, the fish suddenly cast up lungs. Would they be higher or lower? Obviously, they would be lower, because they would drown. They would have a cosmic alienation from the universe that surrounded them.

But man has aspirations; he has what I call his mannishness. He desires that love be more than being in bed with a woman, that moral motions be more than merely sociological something-or-others, that his significance lie in being more than one more cog in a vast machine. He wants a relationship to society or the university other than that of a small machine being manipulated by a big machine. On the basis of modern thought, however, all of these would simply be an illusion. And since there are aspirations which separate man from his impersonal universe, man then faces at the heart of his being a terrible, cosmic, final alienation. He drowns in cosmic alienation, for there is nothing in the universe to fulfill him. That is the position of modern man. There is nothing there to fulfill him in all that there is.

Remember the great cry of the modern artist, the prophet of today, as he cries out about cosmic alienation. Just before his death Alberto Giacometti said: I've never been able to picture the situation of man. If I could, no one could look at it because it would be too horrible. If you go into a good museum where his work is displayed right, there are always huge areas around the individual figures. In Giacometti there is a concept of total loneliness.

Charlie Chaplin also expressed it. In the modern age Chaplin is not the clown, he is the thinker. For modern man, there is no god, there are no angels, no other conscious life in the universe. All the concepts of conscious life in the universe are merely statistical elongation and projection. So when Charlie Chaplin heard that there were no conscious beings on Mars, he said, "I feel lonely." He is the modern philosopher speaking with force. If God is not there, who is there?

Or take Mortimer Adler's book *The Difference of Man and the Difference It Makes.* Adler writes that if we do not soon find a difference with man, we will treat him like a machine. Thousands of the student generation have decided that that is now no longer a prophecy, but a fact. And let me add that we can expect men to be treated like machines if we believe that people are machines.

The situation students face in the universities today can be instructive. Most of their professors have been teaching that man is a machine. The result: Students are being treated like machines. Their reaction is right: Student revolt in this situation is understandable.

modern man as mystic

Let us understand further that modern man could not tolerate being shut up finally into the mere stuff of machinery. And so modern man has become a mystic.

Rousseau and Kant both lead in this direction, but I will start a bit later in history. Kierkegaard is the key. Some may feel that I attribute to Kierkegaard the attributes peculiar to his followers and not to him and, surely, that is a point that could be argued. But whether Kierkegaard or Kierkegaardianism gave birth to it—I think it was Kierkegaard—we now have a divided universe, something man has not faced in past history. Before this, philosophers and thinkers were always striving for a unified field concept, a concept that would include all of life and all of knowledge.

Modern man, however, has accepted a total dichotomy. Beginning with rationalism, rationally you come only to pessimism. Man equals the machine. Man is dead. So Kierkegaard and those who followed him put forth the concept of the non-rational and the hope of an optimism in the area of non-rationality. Faith and optimism, they said, are always a leap. Neither has anything to do with reason.

This new way of looking at knowledge is, I feel, at the heart of the difference between the generations. A middle-class adult, even a teacher who has taught these things but in an abstract way, cannot understand unless he has been down wrestling with those who have themselves wrestled in a consistent way with these matters. In this now accepted dichotomy there is no exchange at all between reason which leads to pessimism and anything which leads to optimism. Any optimism concerning God or beauty, any concept of the significance of man or of moral motions, always has to be in the area of non-reason. This is the situation, therefore, at the heart of the generation gap: Modern man has come to the place where he has given up his rationality in order to hold on to his rationalism.

So modern man, then, holds on to his rationalism (that man should understand the world by starting totally from himself), even though it has led him to give up hope for a unified field of knowledge and to give up confidence in rationality which all men in the past rightly fought for, because God has made man in his own image and a part of this image is reason.

Therefore, modern man is a mystic, but his mysticism is quite different from that of, say, the Roman Catholic mystic of the past. Modern man is a mystic in the sense of his leaping "upstairs"—as I have used this language in *Escape from Reason* and *The God Who Is There.*[3] He seeks optimism on the basis of non-reason. He does not know why he must leap, yet he feels forced to make the leap against his reason.

Christians know why the non-Christian must leap. He must leap because he has been made in the image of God. No matter how far he is separated from God by false intellectual systems and by his guilt and his sin, he has not become non-man. He is still made in the image of God even though he is a rebel and separated from God.

Modern man finds he must leap into the irrational even though he does not know why he must leap. Holding to the uniformity of natural causes in a closed system, he is left with only the impersonal plus time plus chance. This does not explain man's aspirations, and so, feeling really damned, caught in his own kind of hell, he leaps upstairs.

the common man as mystic

This leap began in philosophy, moved into the arts with the post-impressionists, into music after Debussy, into other cultural areas (in the English-speaking world) with T. S. Eliot and finally into theology with Karl Barth. It is the total irrational leap. It spread in various ways: first through the intellectuals, to the educated people; then it swept around the middle class, and it has also influenced the masses through the common media. Toss open *TIME* or *Newsweek,* the British newspapers, *L'Express* or *Der Spiegel* on the Continent, and one sees the message carried down to the common man.

But the movies scream it louder than all. There are two kinds of films—those that merely entertain and those that are the good ones. The good films are the awful ones, because they teach that there is no truth, no meaning, no absolutes, that it is not only that we have not found truth and meaning but that they do not exist.

---

[3] "Upstairs"—"an upper story experience"—is a term used to denote that which, in modern thinking, deals with significance or meaning, but it is not open to contact with verification by the world of facts or reason.

The student and the common man may not be able to analyze it, but day after day, day after day, they are being battered by this concept. We have now had a generation or two of it, and we must not be blind to the fact that it is getting across.

In contrast, this way of thinking has not had nearly as much influence on the middle class. They keep thinking in the old way as a memory of the time before the Christian base was lost in this post-Christian world. However, the majority in the middle class have no real basis whatsoever for their values since they have given up the Christian viewpoint. They just function on the "memory." This is why so many young people feel that the middle class is ugly. These people are plastic, ugly and plastic, because they try to tell others what to do on the basis of their own values, but with no ground for those values. They have no base and they have no categories.

Take, for example, the faculty members who cheer when the student revolt strikes against the administration and who immediately begin to howl when the students start to burn up faculty manuscripts. They have no categories to say this is right and that is wrong. Such people still hang on to their old values by memory, but they have no base for them at all.

Not long ago John Gardner, head of the Urban Coalition, spoke in Washington to a group of student leaders. His topic was on restoring values in our culture. When he finished, there was a dead silence. Then finally one man from Harvard stood up and in a moment of complete brilliance asked, "Sir, upon what base do you build your values?" I have never felt more sorry for anybody in my life. He simply looked down and said, "I do not know." I had spoken that same day about what I am writing in the first part of this book. It was almost too good an illustration of my lecture. Here was a man crying to the young people for a return to values, but he offered nothing to build on; a man who was trying to tell his hearers not to take off for Morocco and yet gave no reason why they should not. Functioning only on a dim memory, these are the parents who have turned off their children when their children ask why and how. When their children cry out, "Yours is a plastic culture," they are silent. We have the response so beautifully stated in the Beatles' *Sergeant Pepper,* "She is leaving home—we gave her everything money could buy." This is the only answer such parents can give.

They are upset by their own or other children taking drugs. They are bothered about what they read in the newspapers concerning the way the country and the culture are going. When they read that there is a porno-

graphic play in New York, such as *Oh Calcutta!* they are distressed—
though if they were to go to New York, and their friends were not around,
they might go to see it just because it is a dirty play. Nevertheless, they
would have a vague unhappiness about it, feel threatened by all of it, and
yet have no base upon which to found their judgments.

And tragically, such people are on every side. They constitute the largest body in our culture—northern Europe, Britain and also in America
and other countries as well. They are a majority—the "Silent Majority"—
but they are weak as water. They are people who like the old ways because
they are pleasant memories, because they give what to them is a comfortable way to live. But they have no basis for their values.

Education, for example, is accepted and pressed upon their children as
the only thinkable thing to do. Success is starting the child at the earliest
possible age and then, within the least possible years, his obtaining a
master's or a Ph.D. degree. Yet if the child screams, Why?, the only
answers are, first, because it gives social status and then because statistics
show that if you have a university or college education, you will make
$10-15,000 more a year. There is no base for real values or even the why
of a real education.

huxley and the drug culture

It would likewise be possible to study the irrational leap toward non-
rational values in existentialism, looking at the three French, German and
Swiss philosophers—Jean-Paul Sartre, Martin Heidegger and Karl Jaspers.
The early Wittgenstein, too, is central. But here I will limit myself to just
one more aspect before discussing the student rebellion in more detail.

That aspect is best seen in Aldous Huxley. You cannot understand the
student generation without understanding him. Huxley is the father of the
modern cult of drug taking. Huxley did not suggest drugs as an escape.
Rather, he said, because reason is not going to take us anywhere, one
could give healthy people drugs and help them have some kind of experience which one could hope would be optimistic.

Huxley never gave up on this. In the last chapter of *The Humanist
Frame,* which was edited by his brother Julian, it is clear that Aldous held
this position to the end. He also made his wife promise that when he was
dying she would give him LSD so he would die in the midst of a trip. This
is the drug world. I have spoken with hundreds of people on drugs, but I
have never met a really serious drug taker (of course, this is not every little
girl who begins to smoke grass simply because everybody around is smok-

ing it) who did not understand that he was following Huxley's concept of the upper story leap, the upper story hope.

modern theology and God-words
Modern theology has not helped us. From Karl Barth on it is an upper story phenomenon. Faith is a totally upstairs leap. The difficulty with modern theology is that it is no different from taking drugs. It is one trip or another. You may try LSD, you can try the modern theology. It makes no difference—both are trips, separated from all reason.

What we are left with is God-words. Students coming out of all kinds of backgrounds are saying, "I'm sick of God-words." And I must respond, "So am I." These theologians have cut themselves off from any concept of propositional, verbalized revelation in the Bible. They are left upstairs with only connotation words and no content. For them any concept of a personal God is dead, and any content about God is dead. They are cut off from any categories of absolute right and wrong and thus they are left with totally situational ethics. That is all. As you listen to him, the modern theologian is only saying what the surrounding consensus is saying, but in theological terms. There is no help here.[4]

john cage and hissing one's self
The irony of such a situation is played up by an event that happened to John Cage, the modern composer who writes music from a theory of chance, random selection. Leonard Bernstein once offered him the New York Philharmonic Orchestra. Cage directed some of his own chance music and when it was over, he started to take his bows and he thought he heard steam escaping from the steam pipes. Then he realized that the musicians were hissing. As John Cage explains it, it must have been a traumatic experience. But I have often thought about what I would like to have said to the musicians there that night. I am sure that if one had had an hour with those musicians, he would have found that most of them really

---

[4] There are four ways that evangelicals have tended to drift unknowingly in this same direction: (1) by saying, "Don't ask questions; just believe," (2) by decreasing the content of their preaching and teaching until at times the modern man hears their message as, "Drop out and take a trip with Jesus," (3) by praising Karl Barth without realizing that he opened the door to the whole of the theology of the leap and (4) by applying to the early chapters of Genesis the same approach that Barth did to the whole Bible; that is, by separating the Bible's statements in regard to space-time history from "religious truth."

believed philosophically exactly what John Cage believes—that the universe begins with the impersonal plus time plus chance. Why were they hissing, then? They were hissing because they did not like the results of their own teaching when they heard it in the medium to which they were sensitive. They were hissing themselves.

A great number of parents and professors are hissing themselves. They do not like what students do. They do not like what that whole generation is doing. But what they do not face is what the musicians did not face—that basically they believe the same things and they are dishonest, or at least not consistent, in not doing what their children do. Their sons and daughters have simply taken what they have taught and carried it to its logical conclusion.

Malcolm Muggeridge has written much that is worthwhile, but to me the most striking thing he ever wrote was the article in the *New Statesman* (March 11, 1966) that showed he had changed his direction from the New Guardian Leftism to the new Malcolm Muggeridge. He called it "The Great Liberal Death-Wish." He simply admitted that he had realized that the goal toward which he had been optimistically moving was not going to be realized. The liberalism in which he had his hopes had cut away all the groundwork and left no categories with which to judge. Muggeridge still feels this strongly: Liberalism has committed suicide because it has cut away its foundation. So the faculty screams with glee when students storm the administrative offices but squeals once they turn against the faculty. They have cut away their own foundations, and they have no categories with which to say what is right and what is wrong, and they have no way to stop the flood they have loosed.

law is king

This is a complete contrast to that upon which government was built in the United States. We had freedom and form, form and freedom. Almost all human discussion can turn upon this frame—form and freedom, in the arts, in government, in society. Of course, we have had in the United States in the past a far from perfect situation and much for which we must say we are sorry. Yet the Northern European Reformation culture has had a form and a freedom that no culture in the world has ever had before—unless it was a few small Greek city states for a few years, and there is a question in my mind concerning that. But the northern European countries built on the Reformation had form and freedom, and there are specific Anglo-Saxon varieties of this: Samuel Rutherford, for example, the great leader of the second Reformation in Scotland and his book, *Rex Lex*. Law is king.

How could law—rather than arbitrary judgments of individuals or an elite—be king? Simply because God had spoken; there was a base upon which to build law. Law is to be seen not as floating on a sociological set of statistics but on a solid foundation. This notion came into the United States constitution largely through Locke. Locke secularized this base, though even he cheated sometimes and quoted from the Gospels. The American constitution rested on *Rex Lex,* toned down through Locke, through such men as Jefferson, and directly through the great Witherspoon.

There is a huge painting by Paul Robert, a Swiss artist from a great family of artists, who painted in the Supreme Court Building in Switzerland just before 1900. Through Hugh Alexander he had become a Christian, and then he began to express his Christianity in his art. When he was asked to paint this tremendous mural on the stairway leading up to the Supreme Court offices, he expressed in painting what Samuel Rutherford placed in magnificent words. The title of the painting is *Justice Instructing the Judges.* In the foreground are all forms of litigation—the wife against the husband, the architect against the builder. Above them stand the Swiss judges with their little white dickeys. How are these people with their little white dickeys going to judge the litigation? A whole sociological theory is opened to question here. Robert's answer is this: Justice (no longer blindfolded with her sword vertical as is common) is unblindfolded with her sword pointing downward to a book on which is written "The Word of God." Here is *Rex Lex,* because justice is not merely statistical averages. Here is something to build on.

Compare this with Wittgenstein's and Bergman's understanding of the problem of silence. In Robert's scheme we are no longer like the fish in the room; no longer do we face cosmic alienation; no longer is there a lack of categories to explain why some things are right and some things are wrong; no reason in such a case why we cannot build without alienation. For there is revelation from outside man—propositional, verbalized revelation. It is not the Christians who have to leap. It is humanistic man who must leap into a mysticism with nothing there.

It is a matter of presuppositions. Many people catch the presuppositions like some children catch childhood diseases. They have no idea where they come from. But that is not the way the thinker chooses his presuppositions. His presuppositions are selected on the basis of which presuppositions fit what is; that is, what presuppositions give solid answers concerning what is. It is only the Christian presuppositions which explain what is—in regard to the universe and in regard to man.

Jesus' answer to camus

Consider further Camus in *The Plague.* Nothing is better for understanding modern man's dilemma. Modern man asks, "Where does justice come from? How can I move?" Camus says, "You can't. You're really damned." The more you feel the tension of injustices, the more your damnation as modern man and the modern rationalist increases. In *The Plague,* which is Camus' center piece, as the rats bring the disease into Oran, Jean Tarrou is faced with a dilemma. He may choose to join with the doctor and fight the plague, in which case he will be humanitarian, but he will be fighting God, in Camus' construction. Or he can join with the priest and refuse to fight the plague and he will be non-humanitarian. And poor Camus died with this dilemma upon him. He never solved it.

In contrast, of course, you have the magnificent account in the Bible. Jesus Christ who is God and claims to be God in the full Trinitarian sense stands in front of the tomb of Lazarus. As he stands in front of the tomb, he is angry. The Greek makes that plain. As Jesus stands there in his anger, we may notice something. The Christ who claims to be God can be angry at the result of the Fall and the abnormal event which he now faces *without being angry at himself.*

It is titanic. Suddenly I can fight injustice knowing I am not fighting what is good. It is not true that what is is right. I can fight injustice knowing there is a reason to fight injustice. Because God does not love everything, because he has a character, I can fight injustice without fighting God.

What a contrast this is to Antonioni's *Blow-up!* This movie is probably the most skillful of all of the philosophic films. Two things are shown in *Blow-up*: first, murder without guilt (in other words, no moral categories) and, second, love without meaning (no human categories).

But the modern mind goes further. It understands that if you abandon these categories, you also abandon the distinction between reality and fantasy—even if you are not on a drug trip. *Juliet of the Spirits, The Hour of the Wolf, Bel de Jour*—all these films are saying the same thing. These are not extreme statements, not just theoretical theses. It is obvious that the thinking process is boiling over into practical results. I am intrigued by the fact that more and more young people come to me and say, "I can no longer be sure of what is real." It is modern man's dilemma.

the context of the student revolt

Here, then, is the context in which the student revolt can be understood. This is how we came to be where we are. Society has reaped the rewards of its escape from reason. From modern science to modern, modern science, from man made in the image of God to man the machine, from freedom within form, to determinism and autonomous freedom, from harmony with God to cosmic alienation, from reason to drugs and the new mysticism, from a biblically based theology to God-words—this is the flow of the stream of rationalistic history. Out of this stream comes the student revolution.

2

the international student revolution

Now that we have seen *how* we got to be where we are, we will look at *where* we are. By what steps did the present student revolt boil up?

It began at Berkeley in the fall of 1964 and there the various student protests tended to take two different but related forms. First, there was the Free Speech Movement that began as an attempt to give students a chance to engage in politically relevant activity—political recruitment, speeches, etc.—on the University campus itself. Within this movement there were students of all shades of political persuasion.

At the same time another element emerged. The hippie movement cried for absolute, autonomous freedom. They stood, whether consciously or not, in the stream of Rousseau, Thoreau, the Bohemian life and hedonism. Any authority was met with the cry of "fascist" or "Cossack." In their definition a fascist or Cossack included anybody who suggested *any* restraint on freedom of the individual. Basically, with these students the rebellion was apolitical. The hippies simply dropped out of society, literally doing nothing much one way or another for or against society. They just opted out.

There was a short-lived third stream as well—the Filthy Speech Movement which had its major fling some months after the Free Speech Movement began. This rebellion took the form of grabbing the microphone and shouting four-letter words into the ears of all within reach of the amplifying system. A rather crazy idea of freedom if you stop to think about it! This stream was important in that it has influenced the vocabulary of much of the present radical rhetoric.

But whether it was the Free Speech people or the hippies (who often were involved with drugs), their first sentence was: "We live in a plastic culture."

This sentence was not wrong, it was right. The evangelical, orthodox church should have been saying it for twenty years. If we had, the young people might not be in the dilemma they are in now. But orthodox Christians had lost the *status quo,* and had hardly noticed that it was gone. Most Christian leaders try to plead with the young people to "maintain the conservative position" without realizing that the conservative position means the majority position or the generally accepted position, and Christians no longer hold the majority position. We who hold to historic Christianity are now an absolute minority.

The only way to reach our young people is no longer to call on them to maintain the *status quo* but to teach them to be revolutionary, as Jesus was revolutionary equally against both Sadducees and Pharisees. In this biblical sense we must be revolutionary. If we are going to say anything to our generation, whether it be for individual conversion or a cultural extension with Christ being Lord of all, we must build upon the understanding that the generation in which we live is plastic. *Plastic* is a good word here, for plastic is synthetic and it also has no natural grain or form. The church has not spoken nearly what God would have it speak. It has acted as though the Christian base could be removed and it would make no practical difference to society, culture, its own young people, or what is needed to live and speak into such a world.

the new industrial state

But, if on one side there was the hippie and the Free Speech Movement, there was yet another. Coming forth at the same time was John Kenneth Galbraith. *The New Industrial State* is the book in which Galbraith clearly stated the direction, though in the Reith Lectures, for example, he had already clearly outlined it. Galbraith, though he does not use the same words, agrees with the hippies that we live in a plastic culture. Culture has lost its way and we should now have somebody new to direct it. Who should direct it? Galbraith's answer was and is: the academic and especially the scientific elite, plus the state. To those who know Plato, it all sounds very familiar. The philosopher kings are to be reinstated.

trouble in utopia

Of course problems arose in both views. Within the hippie and the Free Speech movement one problem was pointed up very early by Allen Ginsberg. He made the shrewdest comment that I think has been given when he, Alan Watts, Gary Snyder and Timothy Leary met together at a symposium in San Francisco during the apex of hippieism. Leary and others were warmly speaking of the virtues of drugs and of the great future coming under the new absolute freedom. On the basis of hedonism we will come to a golden tomorrow. Every man will be personally free, having no restraints. Man, especially under the influence of drugs, is going to come to his utopia. Ginsberg, with all his brilliance, pricked that balloon with a single sentence. He simply said, "But, Tim, somebody must make the posters." The simple fact is that freedom without form produces nothing.

We still have the drop outs, the Woodstock people, thousands upon thousands, in Britain 200,000 gathered on the Isle of Wight. There are many of these people. One must add that, nevertheless, the movement no longer has the drive and force that it had at the beginning. Incidentally, there are thousands of these east of Turkey and in North Africa dying at the end of the drug road.

Then, too, drop outs are becoming a problem for society. Society can only stand so many. If society numbers a thousand, it can easily bear five drop outs, or ten, or twenty, maybe even a hundred. But when the number approaches, say, four or five hundred, society must fight back. Society, as society, will not stand too many because it cannot carry them. The difficulty is that the real drop out is a parasite as far as society is concerned, and after a while society cannot carry the load.

Proof of this is Woodstock itself. In Woodstock there were 400,000 people and the whole festival was financed by a young man of the new mentality whose one and a half million dollars spent for Woodstock came from his Establishment background. We must not forget—the drop out problem will not be tolerated by society when it involves too many.

The fact is that the hippie and the Free Speech movements crying out against the plastic society have put forth a solution which will lead in a direction exactly opposite to that for which they hope. It is going to lead, I am convinced, to a total loss of freedom.

The Galbraith side, however, has its own problems. If we have an academic, scientific, state elite without any controls upon them, without any outside universal to guide them, it will undoubtedly lead in the direction of an Establishment totalitarianism. Please repeat the term, "Establishment elite" in your mind until the term is permanently stuck there.

The problem is that you cannot trust the scientist just because he wears a white coat. It is as simple as that. Inside the coat he is still a man. And he is still a fallen man. Even those who are not Christians should understand enough about people to know you cannot trust them merely because of the color of hat or coat they wear. The best illustration of this is Edmund R. Leach, the anthropologist at Cambridge. But I will reserve for the last chapter a fuller discussion of what he exemplifies—scientific manipulation of facts.

the response of the anarchists

Out of the Free Speech, hippie side there come two other answers. Some, of course, are still dropping out. But there are two other branches. In the first, total freedom leads to a new anarchy. This group of students believes that things have become so bad that they could not possibly be worse.

Therefore, they will destroy everything, and without reason they will hope that out of the ashes of destruction will spring forth something better, simply because it could not be worse. They are the bombers in the cities in the United States. Theirs is a vain, romantic dream. Even though he thinks he is tough, eventually the anarchist is a romantic. He hopes something better will come, though he has no reason so to hope.

the response of the new left

Second, out of the Free Speech and the hippie movements the New Left has come. It derives from what, as I said, Ginsberg pointed out: Someone needs to make the posters. And Herbert Marcuse has pointed the way. Marcuse is the philosopher of the New Left, the one who binds the student movement together over almost the whole world. As Galbraith puts forth the concept of an Establishment totalitarianism, Marcuse puts forth the concept of a Left Wing totalitarianism. This is not a theory, it is now in practice. It explains the change in the campus revolutions from Wisconsin and Columbia onwards. It explains what has happened at the University of Wisconsin, at Columbia University, at the Sorbonne and in West Berlin. One of the leaders of the Sorbonne revolution spoke over the French radio. Another student called up on the phone and said, "Give me a chance to speak." But the answer was "No, just shut up—I'll never give you a chance to speak." The same thing is happening wherever the New Left takes over. Here is the complete opposite to the original Free Speech movement—a few hundred tell thousands they must be still.

Many students live in a halfway house, as it were. They do not believe what their parents believe, they would not defend their parents' values, but neither do they have a base for their own beliefs, nor would they hold them for long if challenged. They have no real system of values and, hence, even in the university, they allow an elite to tell them to be still—and they are. The majority allows the minority to direct and dominate.

Some have quit the New Left because it has dawned on them that they are building a new fascist regime, a new fascism in the sense that an elite without any controls upon it, with no universals to impose upon it, is telling everyone else to shut up and listen to them alone.

We must not delude ourselves. These university movements, whether in West Germany, or Italy, or Tokyo or the United States, are only the pilot plan. They are meant to be the pattern for society. What we have going on is a war and those who are being attacked are often oblivious. Students or revolutionaries can present a revolutionary message on radio and TV—a message which many young people understand—and the announcer simply stands and smiles. He does not realize that these people are not playing games. What is happening, then, on our campuses is not meant for the universities alone—it is meant for the total society.

This, then, is the situation. Whether it is a Left Wing elite or an Establishment elite, the result is exactly the same. There are no real absolutes controlling either. In both cases one is left with only arbitrary absolutes set by a totalitarian society or state with all the modern means of manipulation under its control. Both the Left Wing elite and the rising Establishment elite are a threat.

three alternatives to christianity

Before explaining what I take to be the proper Christian response to the revolution going on today, I wish to summarize the three basic alternatives to that Christian response. If one abandons the Christian solution—the return to the absolutes and universals possible because of God's speaking clearly to man—there are three (and only three) possible alternatives.

The first is hedonism—namely, that every individual does exactly what he wants to do. Hedonism can function as long as you have one man. But as soon as you have more than one person in society, chaos immediately follows. Imagine two hedonists meeting each other over a swift stream on a single log. Here you have the dilemma. But hedonism still holds many young people—the hippie as he was in the beginning, the Free Speech advocate believing he could build on hedonism and it would work. But it hasn't. All you have to do is go to Haight-Ashbury and take a look; here you will see a desert, a desert formed by the hedonism of people who hoped for something better.

The second possibility, if you do not have an absolute, is the dictatorship of 51%, with no controls and nothing with which to challenge the majority. This is sociological law—the law of averages, the law of majority opinion. In the United States, Oliver Wendell Holmes and the Yale University Law School were the first to act upon such open sociological law. The concept of *Rex Lex,* that there is a real base to build on, is gone, and even the constitution is to be viewed as a less than firm form of restraint. The courts make sociological law.

But one must understand where this leads: It means that if Hitler was able to get a 51% vote of the Germans, he had a right to kill the Jews.

Our Christian forefathers who built the Reformation concept of government with its checks and balances did not believe in the dictatorship of

51%. In Scandinavia, Switzerland, Holland, Canada, the United States, there were checks and balances in government. The English had the Crown, the House of Lords, the House of Commons and the Prime Minister and the courts balanced against each other. The Swiss were so insistent on the matter of checks and balances that the Supreme Court building was not even allowed to be in the same city as the rest of the government. Today the Supreme Court is still in Lausanne and the rest of the government in Berne. But in current political thinking—in the absolute power of 51%, law by consensus—all this is laid aside. No longer can the little man with the open Bible say to the 51%, you are wrong. No longer is there an absolute anywhere with which to measure and judge. A shifting and arbitrary consensus rules.

The third possibility is an elite or a dictator, that is, some form of totalitarianism wherein a minority, the elite, or one man tells the society what to do. Again in this case arbitrary absolutes are set up, free from the control of any universal.

I would say it again: If you do not have an absolute that resides somewhere, to which you can appeal, these are the only three sociological possibilities. Our professors did not seem to realize when they cut away the Christian position that it was going to lead to one of these three positions. They destroyed the base and shortsightedly did not know what would follow.

the current situation

What, then, is the situation now? Recognizing that there are a number of variations within general categories, we can still single out four basic groups. First is the hippie, drop out world. Second is the New Left, a left wing totalitarianism centered in a left wing elite with no absolutes to limit their action. The anarchists are ideologically different, but practically they supplement the New Left; the black flag often flies beside the red. Third is the rising Establishment elite. They too have only arbitrary absolutes to limit their action, and therefore their position also leads to force and the loss of liberty. The fourth and largest block are those who in 1970 came to be called the "Silent Majority." They are the majority in the United States, England and many other countries. They can elect whomever they will under our present democratic voting procedures.

This Silent Majority, however, must be clearly understood to have two unequal parts: (1) the Christians, standing in the stream of historic Christianity, living under the propositional revelation of God as he has spoken in the Bible, and therefore having absolutes (These are a minority within the Silent Majority.) and (2) the totally different majority of the Silent Majority who are living on the memory of the practical advantages that Christian culture gave but have no base for these advantages. Their values are affluence (they are practical materialists) and personal peace at any price. Having no base, no absolutes, most of them will compromise liberty any time they are finally forced to choose between their affluence and personal peace on the one hand and giving up of a piece of liberty on the other. They are no closer to the true Christian than are the hippie community and the New Left. In fact, they are probably further away, for they have no values that deserve the name. Affluence and personal peace at any price as the controlling factors of life are as ugly as anything could be.

Another factor is involved here. Many of the drop outs and New Left people are getting disillusioned. They no longer have hope. Take, for example, the music of Bob Dylan and the Beatles. They are no longer shouting, "here is the answer," but have given up the hope of finding answers and are now just making romantic music. The romantic end of Antonioni's *Zabriskie Point* is another case. I am sure parents think that this new music is better than the old, but they are wrong, for all hope is gone out of it.

The drop outs and the New Left people who reach this place then tend to drift into the majority of the Silent Majority. They may continue to smoke grass, but they no longer have any reason to do anything that disturbs their form of peaceful life; they have no ideals to cause them to do anything but drift. Many of the original Berkeley Free Speech people, or people like them, will never again risk anything to speak for free speech.

The result of all this present situation will, I believe, be this. As the New Left grows stronger and more violent and disruptive, and as the number of drop outs who must be carried by society increases, society itself will move further toward chaos. The majority of the Silent Majority then will fight back and in doing so tend to accept the Establishment elite and its solutions, namely a growing Establishment totalitarianism. At first this may not seem to be as serious as the totalitarianism of the New Left, but it is just as much without absolutes and will eventually be as oppressive, even if in a less open way.

The danger is that the evangelical, being so committed to middle-class norms and often even elevating these norms to an equal place with God's absolutes, will slide without thought into accepting the Establishment elite.

the christian response

If this is the situation, what then is the Christian response? Some Christians have supposed that the choice is between a revolutionary stance and some kind of reconciliation. The Christian, it is assumed, is to choose reconciliation. But we cannot have reconciliation in a world like ours unless something happens first. We are headed for the disaster I have described above, and no nice soft talk of reconciliation and the contentless word "love" is going to have any meaning in such a setting. We must have something stronger.

We must have a Christian revolution. Love, yes. But let us understand that if we are to have it, we need to know what it is. We need what the Reformation built on, that which derives from Scripture itself—that God is not only a God of love, but a God of holiness. He is a God with character. Everything is not equally right with God, and because of this we have our absolutes and we have our categories. We are not left with silence as Wittgenstein saw it: God has spoken in propositions to man.

Because God has spoken in a propositional, verbalized way in the Bible, we can have categories, in relationship to knowing—we do not have to be lost between fantasy and reality—to morals, to law and to social action. In this setting man is no longer dead. He has been separated from God by his true moral guilt, but he is not dead. Man is wonderful, made in the image of the personal God. Here is the answer both to Rousseau and to the mechanical world, whether in chemical determinism or psychological determinism. And in the substitutionary death of Christ who died upon the cross in space and time and history, there is a way for our true moral guilt to be removed and for man to return to fellowship with God.

Here, then, is the basis for a revolution built on truth. We can, by God's grace, build again. To young people who want a revolution, I would say this: You cannot be a revolutionary simply by letting your hair grow and growing a beard. To be a real revolutionary you must become involved in a real revolution—a revolution in which you are pitted against everybody who has turned away from God and his propositional revelation to men, against even the users of the God-words, a revolution in which we may again hope to see good results, not only in individuals going to heaven but in Christ who is Lord becoming Lord in fact in this culture of ours to give us even in this fallen world something of both truth and beauty.

cobelligerents, not allies

Let me suggest three implications of what a true revolution will mean in the light of where we are. First, Christians must realize that there is a difference between being a cobelligerent and an ally. At times you will seem to be saying exactly the same thing as the New Left elite or the Establishment elite. If there is social injustice, say there is social injustice. If we need order, say we need order. In these cases, and at these specific points, we would be cobelligerents. But do not align yourself as though you are in either of these camps: You are an ally of neither. The church of the Lord Jesus Christ is different from either—totally different.

My observation among many young pastors and others is this. Suddenly they are confronted by two camps and they are told, "Choose, choose, choose." And by God's grace they must say, "I will not choose. I stand alone with God, the God who has spoken in the Scripture, the God who is the infinite personal God, and neither of your two sides is standing there. So if I seem to be saying the same thing at some one point, understand that I am a cobelligerent at this particular place, but I am not an ally."

The danger is that the older evangelical with his middle-class orientation will forget this distinction and become an ally of the Establishment elite, and at the same time his son or daughter will forget the distinction and become an ally of the New Left elite. We must say what the Bible says when it causes us *to seem to be saying* what others are saying, such as "Justice!" or "Stop the meaningless bombings!" But we must never forget that this is only a passing cobelligerency and not an alliance.

the preaching and the practice of truth

Second, we and our churches must take truth seriously. The great tragedy is that in all our countries evangelicalism under the name of evangelicalism is destroying evangelicalism. Orthodoxy under the name of orthodoxy is destroying orthodoxy. Take the Free University of Amsterdam, that great school that under Abraham Kuyper really spoke for God, not only in theology but in its understanding of culture. Today the Theology Department in the Free University destroys the Scripture. In America it is the same. We have theological seminaries that call themselves evangelical and no longer hold to the Scriptures, especially the first half of Genesis, as fully inspired in regard to its historic content. In England it is the same. T. H. Huxley spoke as a prophet in 1890 when he said that there would come a day not far hence when faith will be separated from all fact (especially all pre-Abrahamic history) and faith will go on triumphant forever. That is where not only the liberal theologians are but also the evangelical, the orthodox theologians who begin to tone down on the truth, the propositional truth of Scripture which God has given us.

The key here is antithesis. If a statement is true, its opposite is not true. We must take this very seriously. Many of us in the name of evangelicalism are letting it slip through our fingers. Unless we accept the modern 20th-century concept that religious truth is only psychological truth, then if there is that which is true, the opposite is not true. Two religions that teach exactly the opposite things may both be wrong, but they cannot both be right. We must act upon, witness and preach this fact: That which is contrary to God's revealed propositional truth is not true, whether it is couched in Hindu terms or traditional Christian terms with new meanings.

All the areas of our personal and corporate life, especially our corporate religious life, must be affected. The early church allowed itself to be condemned, both by the secular and religious authorities. They said, "We must preach, we must witness publicly: We must obey God rather than man." In Acts 4:19-20 they said: In obedience to God, we must say what we have seen, and we must say what we have heard in antithesis to any authority that would tell us to be quiet. They were the practicers of antithesis.

Students from the London School of Economics, Harvard, the Sorbonne, from Africa and Asia and from the ends of the earth have come to L'Abri with their packs on their backs and their long hair and their beards. If you think they would listen to us speak if we were not willing to say that what Christianity teaches, what God has spoken, stands in an antithesis to what is the opposite to what it says, you do not understand your own children or your own age. Our credibility is already minus 5 if we do not say what is false and wrong in contrast to what is true and right. It is minus 430 if we are not willing to stand in the arena of antithesis.

But if first we must speak Christianity with a clear content and an emphasis on truth in contrast to what is not true, equally we must practice truth. This was my stress in my speech to the Berlin Congress on Evangelism, "The Practice of Truth."

We must practice the truth even when it is costly. We must practice it when it involves church affiliation or evangelistic cooperation. There is a difference between having a public discussion with a liberal theologian and inviting him to pray in our program.

This is a time to show to a generation who thinks that the concept of truth is unthinkable that we do take truth seriously by considering the principle of the purity of the visible church and what discipline in regard to both life and doctrine means. We may differ at certain points in application, but the concepts must be discussed and practiced under the leadership of the Holy Spirit. Two biblical principles are to be considered in their interrelationship: (1) The principle of the purity of the visible church and (2) the principle that the world has a right to judge whether we are Christians and whether the Father sent the Son, on the basis of observable love shown among all true Christians.[1]

If we practice latitudinarianism either individually or corporately in an age like our own, we have removed our credibility to the non-Christian, post-Christian, relativistic, skeptical, lost world.

If you think that the tough young people who have rejected the plastic culture and are sick of hypocrisy are going to be impressed when you talk about truth as you unwittingly practice untruth, you are wrong. They will never listen. You have cut the ground from under yourself. We live in a generation that does not believe that such a thing as truth is possible, and if you practice untruth while talking about truth, the real thinkers among the young will just say, "Garbage!"

true christian community

Third, our churches must be real communities. With an orthodoxy of doctrine there must equally be an orthodoxy of community. Our Christian organizations must be communities in which others see what God has revealed in the teaching of his Word. They should see that what has happened in Christ's death and reconciliation on the cross back there in space and time and history is relevant, that it is possible to have something beautiful and unusual in this world in our communication and in communities in our own generation. We may preach truth. We may preach orthodoxy. We may even stand against the practice of untruth strongly. But if others cannot see something beautiful in our human relationships, if they do not see that, upon the basis of what Christ has done, our Christian communities can stop their bickering, their fighting and their in-fighting, then we are not living properly.

The Christian community and the practice of that community should cut across all lines. Our churches have largely been preaching points and activity generators. Community has had little place. In the New Testament church this practiced community was not just a banner but cut all the way down into the hard stuff of the material needs of the members of the community. This was the reason for the appointing of the first deacons. It was also practiced at long distance; the Gentiles of Macedonia, for exam-

---

[1] See the appendix, "The Mark of the Christian."

ple, gave to the needy Jewish Christians in Jerusalem. Such gifts were not considered less spiritual than those gifts sent to Paul to help him in his missionary preaching. Such gifts were not forced; they were made on the basis of free loving community, but they were made as normal among the Christians. This was a practiced orthodoxy of community.

Across *all* lines: I shall never forget the prayer of a young person at the close of my last lecture at Buck Hill Falls. She prayed, "Forgive me for hating adults." May God forgive us, the orthodox of all kinds and ages, for the lack of integration in the Christian groups, across *all kinds* of lines.

I want to see us treating each other like human beings, something that the humanistic student rebels desire but have been unable to produce. Every Christian church, every Christian school, every mission should be a community which the world may look upon as a pilot plant.

When a big company is going to put several million dollars into building a plant, it first builds a pilot plant to show it can be done. Every Christian community everywhere ought to be a pilot plant to show that we can have horizontal relationships with men and that this can result in a community that cares not only for Man with a capital "M" but for the individual, not only for upper case Human Rights but for the whole man in all his needs.

Unless people see in our churches not only the preaching of the truth but the practice of the truth, the practice of love and the practice of beauty; unless they see that the thing that the humanists rightly want but cannot achieve on a humanist base—human communication and human relationship—is able to be practiced in our communities, then let me say it clearly: They will not listen and they should not listen.

true revolution

But if Christians can take these factors into account—(1) the difference between being a cobelligerent and an ally, (2) the preaching and the practice of truth even at great cost in our Christian groups and (3) the observation of community within those churches and Christian groups that stand under the Scripture and for the Word of God—then we will have the possibility of a stirring of a fresh revolution. It will be a real revolution—a real reformation and revival in the orthodox evangelical church. And then by God's grace a Christian consensus may be active again.

We do not need 51% of the people to begin to have an influence. If 10% of the American or English population were really regenerate Christians, clear about their doctrines, beliefs and values, taking truth seriously, taking a consistent position, we could begin, not to have the overwhelming consensus, but at least to have a voice again in the midst of our community. But if this reformation and revival, this positive revolution, does not occur, if we do not begin to put a base back under our culture, the base that was there in the first place and now is so completely gone, then I believe with all my heart and soul that we will have a revolution from either the Left or the Establishment side.

And if this revolution comes from either side, our culture will be changed still further. The last remnants of Christian memory in the culture will be squashed out, and freedoms will be gone. If the revolution comes from the Establishment, it will be much more gradual, much less painful for the Christian—for a while. But eventually it will be as total. We must not opt for one as against the other just because it seems to give a little peace for a little time. That is an enormous mistake because both are equally non-Christian and eventually both will be equal in smashing out the freedoms which we have had.

3

the church in a dying culture

s there a future for the church in the midst of the 20th century? That question is foremost in the minds of young Christians and many older ones as well.

In the previous chapter I have set forth three things that are necessary if the church of the Lord Jesus Christ is to be a revolutionary force in the midst of 20th-century upheaval and revolution: (1) the church must distinguish between being a cobelligerent and an ally, (2) it must be careful to stand clearly for truth, both in doctrine and in practice even when it is costly and (3) it must be more than merely a preaching point and an activity generator; it must show a sense of community.

the truth of christianity

Now I wish to look more closely at the third point—the individual Christian and the Christian community. But even this very practical consideration is built firmly on the basis of the second point mentioned above—the stress on truth in doctrine and practice.

There will be little meaning concerning Christian community until we understand what *Christian* means, and who can make up a Christian community.

The liberal theologians in their stress on community speak and act as though we *become* Christians when we enter the horizontal relationship of community, but this is a totally wrong starting point. If this were so, Christianity would have no more final value than the humanistic community, and that is just the trouble with modern man. He can find no sufficient value for humanistic community for he can find no sufficient value for the men who make it up. If the individual man is a zero, then community is only adding zeros.

We must hold to the great Reformation concepts, and Reformation creeds, and the orthodox creeds prior to these, back to the one that we often recite together—the Apostle's Creed, and then the Nicene Creed, or to the Calcedonian concept of Christology. All these we must hold to, but this is not the final concept of truth the Bible puts forth. The final great concept of truth is that Christianity is true to what is there.

I often think that one of the reasons there is such an air of unreality in much of the church, and for many people, is that they do not understand what is really meant when we say Christianity is true. It is not that it is merely true to a creed, though we should be true to our creeds. It is not even that it is true to the Bible, though certainly our Christianity should be true to the full inspiration of Scripture. But it is rather that Christianity is true to what is really there. It explains why the universe is here and why it has its complexity and its form. It gives us the truth about who man is and the great requirement, the truth that God is there. It tells us that the final environment is not impersonal, but personal. We have an intellectual knowledge which in the middle of the 20th century we can hold with intellectual integrity.

But this knowledge must be practical. Our knowledge concerning the existence of God should flow on into an adoration of this God with our whole selves, including the intellect. Christianity is not only a scholasticism, but, I would insist strongly, it is the highest and the only true mysticism, because it is the only mysticism that allows a man to come into contact with God as a whole man without leaving the intellect hanging outside. And it will not do merely to understand this, but it must flow on in practice individually and then corporately.

the God who is there

Both the individual's and the community's life turns upon the existence of a personal relationship with God. Everything hangs on this point. There will be no reality either in our individual or corporate Christian living and spiritual life except on the basis of a personal relationship with the God who is there. And any concept of a really personal relationship with the God who is there turns upon the fact that God exists and is personal and that I, a man, am made in his image and therefore I am personal. God is infinite. I am finite. But if he is personal and I am personal, made in his image, it is not unnatural that I should be in a personal relationship with the God who is there.

Let us understand that the beginning of Christianity is not salvation: It is the existence of the Trinity. Before there was anything else, God existed as personal God in the high order of Trinity. So there was communication and love between the persons of the Trinity before all else. This is the beginning.

The naturalness of my individual relationship with God does not turn upon the fact of salvation; it turns upon who God is and who I am. Now to enter into this relationship we must have salvation. But the relationship of an individual man, though finite, to the infinite God who is there should never take us by surprise. This is the kind of God we have, and this is the kind of man he has made in his image, distinct from the trees, the plants and the machine-like portion of the universe.

The first commandment is to love God with all our heart, soul and mind. This commandment was not merely spoken by Jesus, but written in the Old Testament, and surely represents the purpose of man's existence— to love God. But it is a meaningless command unless we understand the kind of God who is there and the kind of man that I am.

The theologian who talks about loving God and has no real certainty of any correlation between his use of the word *God* and God's being there is talking nonsense. It is ridiculous to speak of loving a God who is not there. Take, for example, the liberal theologian who says there is no reality in prayer. Bishop Robinson in *Honest to God* shows this clearly in his notion that there is no real vertical relationship with God. It is impossible to have such a relation with God simply because God, for Robinson, is not the kind of God who would make a vertical relationship have any meaning. But God is a personal God, and therefore the call to love him is not nonsense.

Or, on the other hand, take the humanist who thinks man is a machine. If I am a machine, whether chemically or psychologically determined, then my loving God has no meaning. Furthermore, if God is the great philosophic other, or the impersonal everything, pantheism in some sense, then the call to love God is either an illusion or a cruel hoax.

Everything that Christianity has ever had turns on the existence and character of God and the existence and nature of man—the existence and nature of "me." Therefore, the adequate base for individual and corporate Christian living is a personal relationship with the God who is there and who is personal.

Furthermore, how we function must witness to the fact that we know God is there. All too often we say God exists and then go on in just a scholastic orthodoxy. Often, as far as the world can see, our whole organizational program is set up as though God isn't there and we have to do everything ourselves on a Madison Avenue basis.

Suppose we awoke tomorrow morning and we opened our Bibles and found two things had been taken out, not as the liberals would take them out, but *really* out. Suppose God had taken them out. The first item missing was the real empowering of the Holy Spirit and the second item, the reality of prayer. Consequently, following the dictates of Scripture, we would begin to live on the basis of this new Bible in which there was nothing about the power of the Holy Spirit and nothing about the power of prayer. Let me ask you something: What difference would there be from the way we acted yesterday? Do we really believe God is there? If we do, we live differently.

the guilt of man

Of course we know, as we look across mankind and as we look in our own hearts, that man is not what he was originally made to be. I must acknowledge that individually I have deliberately sinned, deliberately done what I know to be wrong. And if I am to be in the place for which I was naturally made, that is, in a personal relationship with this God who exists, something is needed in order to remove this true moral guilt which I have.

The Bible speaks to the man without the Bible—the man who is totally untrained in its content—and it speaks to the man with the Bible—the man who has had intimate exposure to its message. In both cases, it speaks of the fact that all men have individually sinned and as such are under moral guilt before God. This is a tremendous contrast to 20th-century thinking in which man has guilt feelings but no true moral guilt because there are no absolutes before which a man is, or can be, morally guilty. Guilt feelings are all that are possible. But, biblically, all men stand truly morally guilty before God because each has deliberately sinned.

In the first four chapters of Romans, Paul speaks to the Greek and the Roman world, which was very much like our own world both in intellectual intensity and in decadence. There he lays out why a man needs to be a Christian and how he may become one. From the fifth chapter on, Paul speaks to Christians as Christians. The intriguing thing is that it is in the fifth chapter where he is speaking to Christians that he introduces Adam and Adam's revolt against God in order to explain to the Christian the origin of sin in the world. When he talks to the non-Christians in the first chapters and tells them why they should understand that they have true moral guilt, he points out that they have individually and deliberately done those things that they knew were wrong.

Thus in Romans 1:32–2:3 Paul speaks to the man without the Bible: "Who knowing the judgment of God, that they which commit such things are worthy of death, not only do the same, but have pleasure in [consent with] them that do them. Therefore, thou art inexcusable, O man, whosoever thou art that judgest: for wherein thou judgest another, thou condemnest thyself; for thou that judgest doest the same things. But we are sure that the judgment of God is according to truth against them which commit such things. And thinkest thou this, O man, that judgest them which do such things, and doest the same, that thou shalt escape the judgment of God?"

Let me again use an illustration I have used in other places. If every little baby that was ever born anywhere in the world had a tape recorder hung about its neck, and if this tape recorder only recorded the moral judgments with which this child as he grew bound other men, the moral precepts might be much lower than the biblical law, but they would still be moral judgments. Eventually these men come to that great moment when they all stand before God as judge. Suppose, then, that God simply touched the tape recorder button and each man heard played out in his own words all those statements by which he had bound other men in moral judgment. He could hear it going on for years—thousands and thousands of moral judgments made against other men, not aesthetic judgments, but moral judgments. Then God would simply say to the man, though he had never heard the Bible, now where do you stand in the light of your own moral judgments? The Bible points out in the passage quoted above that every voice would be stilled. All men would have to acknowledge that they have deliberately done those things which they knew to be wrong. Nobody could deny it.

We sin two kinds of sin. We sin one kind of sin as though we trip off the curb, and it overtakes us by surprise. We sin a second kind of sin when we deliberately set ourselves up to fall. And no one can say he does not sin in the latter sense. Paul's comment is not just theoretical and abstract, but addressed to the individual—"O man"—any man without the Bible as well as the man with the Bible.

In Romans 2:17 he speaks to the man with the Bible and says the same thing. God is completely just. A man is judged and found wanting on the same basis on which he has tried to bind other men.

the necessity of judgment

But let me stress this warning—it is more than just. It is necessary. It is the only message that is able to speak into the 20th-century mentality because it is the only message which really gives an answer to the two great problems of all men—modern man and man throughout the ages. First, man needs absolutes, universals, something by which to judge.

If one has no basis on which to judge, then reality falls apart, fantasy is indistinguishable from reality, there is no value for the human individual and right and wrong have no meaning.

There are two ways to get away from God's judgment of men. One is to say that there is no absolute. But one must be aware that if God does not judge on a 100% basis, he is indeed like an old man in the sky. And worse—not only is man left in relativism, but God himself is bound by relativism. God must be the judge whose own character is the law of the universe or we have no absolute. We do not need to be embarrassed as we speak of the individual coming to God to be judged in the full historic sense of judgment. It is quite the other way. If this is not true, then we no longer have an absolute, and we no longer have an answer for 20th-century man.

The other way to get away from God's judgment of the individual is to take away the significance of man, to say that he is a machine, or that he is chemically or psychologically determined, that his actions in this world are not his own. In such a case, of course, he is not responsible and cannot be justly judged. But a true significance is the second need of man, and if man is not really significant, then in the name of Christianity we have plunged man back again into the caldron of 20th-century thought where man becomes zero.

My point is simply this. The individual is not separated from God by creation. It is natural that he should be in personal relationship with God; he is separated from God because of his rebellion against God, and there-fore we must stress the solution which the Scripture gives.

christianity's way out

What then is this solution? Paul says it is the same for both the man without the Bible and the man with the Bible. Here is an amazing solution for the problem of man. It only fails to be amazing if we have heard it so long that we simply do not listen. But if you could imagine yourself suddenly coming face to face with this answer for the first time, so that you were not turned off by evangelical phraseology but really were caught by the full force of God's solution to the real dilemma, man's true guilt, you would understand that the word *amazing* is not too strong.

"For I am not ashamed of the gospel of Christ: for it is the power of God [the Greek word is *dynamis,* the dynamite of God, the explosive power of God] unto salvation to every one that believeth; to the Jew first, and also to the Greek" (Romans 1:16). Paul enlarges in Romans 3:23-26: "For all have sinned, and come short of the glory of God." Remember to whom Paul is speaking—the intellectual and sophisticated Greek and Roman world. "For all have sinned, and come short of the glory of God." It is stronger in the Greek—for all have sinned (in the past) and they are falling short (in the present) of the glory of God. But they are "justified freely [*gratis*]."

There is no humanistic note added to salvation here. Man keeps trying to add a humanism to salvation. Whether it is the Judaizers at the time of

Paul, or the classical Roman Catholic Church with the addition of works, or the modern theologian—it does not matter. Man always tries to sneak a humanistic element into salvation. But in the area of individual salvation Scripture rejects all humanism. Man is justified freely "through the redemption that is in Christ Jesus: whom God hath set forth to be a propitiation through faith in his blood, to declare his righteousness for the remission of sins that are past, through the forbearance of God; to declare, I say, at this time his righteousness: that he might be just, and the justifier of him which believeth in Jesus."

Talk about the atom bomb! This is totally explosive—into the midst of the humanism of any age and expressly into the humanism of the 20th century. All too often we pass by this 26th verse too lightly: "To declare, I say, at this time his righteousness: that he [himself] might be just, and [yet] the justifier of him which believeth in Jesus." God keeps his absolute standard and yet there is a way for the individual to be reconciled to him, to be in a personal relationship to him which gives meaning to life. It is at this point that the individual is understood to be the complete contrary of a zero.

somebody knows my name

Christ's death does not leave us with an impersonal relationship to God. Salvation is not merely a magnificent theological or intellectual formula; it is this, but it is much more. The Good Shepherd knows the sheep by name.

Many Christians have heard this for 50 or 60 years, and when they read it again they are half asleep. But there are those also who are inhabitants from the midst of the 20th century, who live in a world of silence, a world in which no one speaks, the world of the early Wittgenstein and Bergman, a world in which there is a desperate longing for communication and love, a world in which no one is there. To these people, I would say, "The Good Shepherd knows the sheep by name. One who becomes a Christian is not merely an IBM card."

Those students who are caught in the great universities and feel the impersonality of the great machine of society and the university manipulating the little machine, can they not understand that here is an entirely different thing? Somebody knows your name in that great crowd. Somebody knows your name as you protest against the IBM machine and the computer-controlled university and society. Because he is infinite, he can know each one personally as though no one else were there. Because the

Good Shepherd is truly a man, but more than a man (the second person of the Trinity and has been for ever), he, being infinite, can know each one personally as though no one else were there.

When by God's grace I accept Christ as my Savior, my Messiah, my real moral guilt before God is gone and I am returned to the place for which I was created—a person-to-person relationship with a personal God. This is vertical personal relationship. Now I can say, "Abba, Father." *Abba* is simply a transliteration from the Aramaic. *Father* is the Greek. In Greek *father* can signify either a gentle or an austere father. But *Abba* is a word that will not allow this. *Abba* is *papa, daddy.* If it is done with reverence, the personal God, the Creator of the universe, may now be spoken of as Papa, as Daddy, whatever your favorite word is for father. You may call him that as long as you come in his way, the non-humanist way, through the finished substitutionary work of Christ as he died in space and time on the cross, and as you do it with awe and reverence.

What we have here is a tremendous personal relationship with the Father—a tremendous father-to-son relationship. Now when I say "Our Father who art in heaven," it is not a figure of speech. (The liberals tell me it is, but it is not.) It is reality. He is my father. I may call him Daddy. I may call him Papa.

The universe is no longer silent and impersonal now. There is someone there who loves me, and I may speak and he hears. Together we may speak, and he as the personal God hears, and he, not being a part of the machine, can work in space and time, back into history, on the basis of our prayer.

Suddenly the great syndrome of the 20th century is smashed. I live now in a different universe, a different world.

Notice, then, that the three problems of modern man fall into place upon this analysis and this solution. First, God is really holy: Absolutes do exist. Second, all men do not need to be lost. Third, man is significant. He is not a stick or a stone, not merely a programmed computer. Here you have suddenly brought together the three explosive answers which modern man really needs.

But it is not only an answer to the needs of the 20th-century man; it is God's solution to the basic problem of all time. Man has been separated from God not by creation, but by rebellion. And God has given a solution that should get us all really excited. This is the only thing finally sufficient to turn us on. I am sick and tired of the evangelical orthodoxy that has ceased to be excited with our answer.

communication and the individual

The first step in understanding Christian community, then, is understanding the individuals who make up the community, for the individual is important to God. And the individual is important to the individual. Christ is not interested simply in a faceless mass.

Because God is personally interested in individual men, he has given them knowledge, knowledge which the individual man desperately needs and may have. God has given it in propositional, verbalized communication in the Bible. And that should not be surprising. It is only astonishing if you fail to remember who man is: Man has been made in the image of God. God has made him to communicate horizontally with other men on the basis of verbalization, and so it is not surprising that the personal God would communicate to him in verbalized form.

Even the toughest atheist agrees that this is not surprising if you begin at the Christian point of beginning. If there is a personal God on the high order of the Trinity so that communication has existed for all eternity, and if he has made man in his own image to be the verbalizer (and, by the way, all modern anthropology so marks man—this is the clearest distinction between man and non-man), then it is not surprising that he would give us true information on the basis of verbalization.

God has given us two kinds of propositional revelation in the Bible. First, didactic statements and commands. Second, a record of how he himself has worked in space-time history. With these two together we really have a very adequate knowledge, both as knowledge and as a basis for action.

God has not given us exhaustive knowledge, but he has given us true knowledge—about himself and about the space-time cosmos. Let me repeat: It is not exhaustive knowledge, but it is true knowledge.

Furthermore, Jesus came as prophet, priest and king. He is the giver of knowledge; he is the revealer of the Godhead bodily. But we must beware lest we begin to make a distinction between the knowledge which Jesus gives and the knowledge which the Bible gives. Jesus himself will not allow any dichotomy here. Jesus says he is the giver of knowledge, but he always quotes the Scripture as though it were also a statement of knowledge to the individual. The Bible and the testimony of Christ stand side by side. What we have here, then, is a person-to-person imparting of knowledge.

christian community

Now we are ready to start talking about the community. I would stress again, however, that a person does not come into relationship with God when he enters the Christian community, whether it is a local church or any other form of community. As I have said, the liberals have gone on to promote other concepts of community. They teach that the only way you can be in relationship to God is when you are in a group. The modern concept is that you enter into community; in this community there is horizontal relationship; in these small I-thou relationships you can hope that there is a big I-Thou relationship.

This is not the Christian teaching. There is no such thing as a Christian community unless it is made up of individuals who are already Christians who have come through the work of Christ. One can talk about Christian community till one is green, but there will be no Christian community except on the basis of a personal relationship with the personal God through Christ. The Christian community is made up of those whom the Good Shepherd knows by name as his sheep, those who are in relationship with God, who stand in a living way as a branch to the vine, the bride to the bridegroom, those who have come to the living God through the work of Jesus Christ as he died upon the cross.

This is the difference between the sacraments of baptism and the Lord's Supper. Baptism is once for all. It represents a man's acceptance of Christ as Savior and then being baptized at that moment with the Holy Spirit. It is a once-for-all situation. The Lord's Supper is taken constantly because it represents the feeding upon Christ which should be constant, moment by moment—to use the modern word, existential. These are the ones who should be making up the Christian community.

We have looked carefully at the individual as he stands in relationship to God. The community stands in the same place. I think we have failed here. We have had a fixed, static concept of the church, that somehow or other the church is not a breathing reality. But even though Christianity is individual, it is not individualistic. One must come to God as an individual, but after we have come one at a time, God does not make us to be horizontally alone.

The first thing God did after he made man was to create someone who would be his counterpart—Eve, different from himself and yet his counterpart—so that there would be a proper, horizontal, finite, personal relationship as well as the vertical personal relationship with the infinite-personal Creator. That is what God wants. God has called us in the New Testament—the Old as well, but in a slightly different form—to come into an understanding that there is to be community, a relationship between those who are already Christians.

Note this: You can have individual Christians and no Christian community, but you cannot have a Christian community without having individual Christians. On the other hand, as evangelical orthodox men and women, we can understand and fight for the need of the individual coming to God and then we can stand individualistically, in a poor sense, rather than in a practicing community. But we must not stand in sheer individualism: Once we are Christians there should be community. As I have used the term before, there is to be an orthodoxy of community as well as an orthodoxy of doctrine.

There are, of course, many forms of Christian communities—local churches, theological schools, Christian colleges, missions, etc. All of these are, or should be, Christian communities, though differing slightly in form. However, they are not entirely equal because, except for the local church, all the others have been chosen by man in the changing needs of the years. In the New Testament, however, the church form has been commanded by God himself for the era in which we live, that is, until Christ's return.

existential living

But regardless of its outward form, the Christian community as a community should understand that *its* first relationship is not horizontal, but vertical. The Christian community is made up of those who are in a personal relationship with God, and then the community *as a unit* is to strive to be first of all in a relationship with God. Its first job is not toward the lost, though it has a task there. The first thing the Christian community should do is to stand *as a community* in a living, existential, moment-by-moment relationship to God. The congregation, the Christian college student body, the family, whatever the community is, this fellowship of believers should stand in awe and worship waiting before God.

Do we really do this? All too frequently as soon as we get together we function like the Board of Trade. Not long ago I was talking to a man whose family owns great cotton mills in England. He said, "You're right. You're right. I go to two kinds of meetings—Christian meetings among Christian brothers, and business meetings at the cotton mill. Sometimes I suddenly sit up in the middle of the meeting and ask myself, 'Which meeting am I in?' "

Community relationship to God does not come mechanically. Even when a group stands for the purity of the visible church and for the historic Christian faith, it does not mean that we, *as a group*, mechanically and automatically practice a relationship upward to God. It is something that must be consciously and continuously sought after. The individual, and then the group, must consciously look to Christ for help, consciously look to the leadership of the Holy Spirit not only theoretically but in reality, consciously understanding that every relationship must first be toward God before it has meaning out toward men. And only after the vertical relationship—first individually and then as the group—is established are we ready to have horizontal relationships and a proper Christian community. It is a long way to come. But there is no other way to achieve authenticity.

But as we come now as a community consciously realizing our calling, we can know who we are in our horizontal relationships. First of all, to these around me in my Christian community, I am a man among men. I am one flesh, one blood with them. They are made in the image of God, and I am made in the image of God. We have one Creator—one origin. Second, I am a brother in Christ with them because they and I, by God's grace, have come under the finished work of Jesus Christ.

Therefore, as we meet in our groups, we know who we are. We are not like those who march in our streets and do not know who they are—who call for community but have no basis for community beyond biological continuity. Now we are ready to begin real personal living, to practice the orthodoxy of community corporately as a community. Real personal Christian living individually and corporately as a community that rests upon the individual's and the community's personal relationship with a personal God gives us the possibility of Christian community before the eye of an observing world. But there is no use taking all this time, this whole chapter, to understand what Christian community is if we do not practice it! We will continue through the remainder of this book to think about what that practice means in the midst of our dying culture.

4

form and freedom in the church

We now come to the fourth consideration needed if the church is going to be what it should be, ready for what lies ahead in the years at the end of the 20th century. The first is the difference between being a cobelligerent and an ally. The second, the preaching and practice of truth, even if at great cost. The third, the practice of the orthodoxy of community within the true Christian groups and between true Christian groups. The fourth is the consideration of what form and what freedom the Bible gives in regard to the church as the church, or we could speak of it as the boundary conditions set forth in the New Testament on the polity of the church.

Note that here we are not just speaking of Christian work in general but the church as the church—what is often spoken of today as the institutional organized church. Does *it* have a future?

The church of Jesus Christ is, of course, first of all the church invisible. It is the body of believers united by faith in Christ in the full biblical sense, whether or not they are members of an external organization. It includes the church today at war in the present world and the church of yesterday whose members are already at peace. It is the church universal. When Jesus said, "I will build my church" (Matthew 16:18), this was what he meant. And the writer of Hebrews, in 12:22-23, had the same thing in mind—the unity of the entire body of believers of all times and all places.

the visible church

But one of Jesus' remarks also points to the visibility of the church. In Matthew 18:17 Jesus says, "And if he shall neglect to hear them, tell it unto the church: but if he neglect to hear the church, let him be unto thee as an heathen man and a publican." So here we have already indicated the fact that the church is not only to be invisible, but visible as well. It would be meaningless to command to bring before the invisible church a brother in Christ with whom we have had a difference. There is an indication here that there is some structure to which we may bring our brother when we have had a falling out—a structure which makes a distinction between those in that structure and those out of it.

As we turn to the book of Acts we find this concept is immediately picked up and carried out very rapidly. Acts 13:1-2 concerns the group of Christians at Antioch. Antioch is a place of importance because it is the place where most church historians and exegetes feel that for the first time full Gentiles (not just "God fearers," Gentiles like Cornelius who believed but had not taken on the full Jewish rites) were reached by the Christian Jews.

The text begins: "Now there were in the church that was at Antioch. . . ." Thus, here was a functioning local congregation called "the church." From here on the New Testament clearly indicates that churches were formed wherever some became Christians.

Salvation, as I have emphasized already, is individual, but not individualistic. People cannot become Christians except one at a time, and yet our salvation is not solitary. God's people are called together in community. Hence at Antioch individual Christians are not now acting individualistically; they are acting as a unit.

Not only the officers among the believing Jews but apparently the members at Antioch as well could not refrain from telling the good news to their Gentile neighbors. Manaen especially is singled out and called, according to the best translation, "Herod's foster brother." Here, then, is a member of the aristocracy who was a member of the church at Antioch.

This church covered the whole spectrum of society. It was as wide as the culture which it faced. Undoubtedly it had simple people in it, but it could also have Herod's foster brother. It had Jews, and it had Gentiles. It was, in fact, from the very beginning the ideal local church. It encompassed the whole spectrum of the surrounding society, including, furthermore, those who, like Herod's foster brother and a slave, could not come together in any other setting.

Similarly, you will notice that though they were not all "professional ministers" or "missionaries," yet they were all tellers. Christians felt a burden for being tellers into their own culture, and this is how the Gentiles became Christians here at Antioch. But also they felt a burden for sending Paul and Barnabas abroad.

In a sense we have a complete picture of what the local church ought to be: Individuals were becoming Christians, but not individualistic ones; the congregation covered the full spectrum of the society; the members were all tellers, not only at home but abroad. And when the Holy Spirit said that Barnabas and Saul should be sent on the first missionary journey, the members did not function only as individual Christians, but as a unit, as a church.

I am often asked, "Is the institutional church finished as we face the end of the 20th century?" My answer is very much No, for the church is clearly given as a New Testament ordinance until Christ returns. However, that is a very different thing from forgetting that the New Testament gives freedoms as well as forms as to what the institutional church may be like.

Let us consider what limits the New Testament places upon the institutional church; that is, what form the New Testament imposes. We have already dealt with the command for orthodoxy of doctrine and life and orthodoxy of community. Now we are thinking of the New Testament statements concerning the polity of the church as a church. *The first of these is that local congregations are to exist and that they are made up of Christians.*

the formation of local churches

If we look on into Acts 16:4-5, we hear about the missionary journey upon which Paul and Barnabas had been sent from the church at Antioch. "And as they went through the cities, they delivered them the decrees for to keep, that were ordained of the apostles and elders which were at Jerusalem. And so were the churches established in the faith, and increased in number daily." As the missionary journey progressed, once more individuals were brought to salvation, but they soon joined together in a specific, observable structure, an organization with form. Throughout Paul's missionary journey we see a stress on the formation of churches.

In Romans 16:16 Paul writes, "Salute one another with an holy kiss. The churches of Christ salute you." The reference is to churches, not just the church. In II Corinthians 11:28, Paul refers to "the care of all the churches." Romans 16:3-4 contains some very instructive statements about the early churches that were formed. "Greet Priscilla and Aquila." (In Greek the word is *Prisca,* a term of fondness for Priscilla.) "Greet Prisca and Aquila my helpers in Christ Jesus: who have for my life laid down their own necks: unto whom not only I give thanks, but also all the churches of the Gentiles." It is not *church,* but *churches*; individual churches were formed.

Paul continues, "Likewise greet the church that is in their house." Aquila and Priscilla were then in Rome. But when they were in Asia, as we learn in I Corinthians 16:19, they also had a church in their home. Apparently wherever Priscilla and Aquila went, people were saved and a church was then started.

It is interesting, however, that the church was in their home. Lightfoot says that there were no church buildings as such before the third century. Since Lightfoot made that statement, however, archaeologists have found a most interesting place in Rome. Roman houses—unless they were the great mansions—were relatively small. What archaeologists found was a place with the facade of two houses still untouched, but with the internal walls torn out to make a larger room. And from everything that was found there, the archaeologists believe that this was a church building. This structure is dated at the end of the second century. But whether one accepts Lightfoot's beginning in the third century, or whether one dates it at the end of the second century, it really makes no difference. There is no biblical norm as to where and where not the church should meet. *The central fact is that the early concept of the church had no connection with a church building.* The church was something else: a group of Christians drawn together by the Holy Spirit in a place where they worked together in a certain form, a form which we will examine as we go now through various verses in the New Testament.

I Corinthians 4:17 and 7:17 also give the most clear statements that one could have that churches were considered as churches and not just as an abstract or invisible concept. Individual churches were formed as people became Christians and these were definite, specific entities.

In I Corinthians 11:18, we have a note which is unhappy, and yet which is surely encouraging for us. "First of all when ye come together in the church, I hear that there be divisions among you; and I partly believe it." It is unfortunate and yet it is encouraging to us that already at this early time we find troubles and problems in the church. The church is not a church building, mind you, but a congregation of believers. And this congregation of believers was not perfect because there is nothing perfect in a fallen world. And Christians are not perfect until Jesus comes. So while there is discipline in the church, this does not mean that something is held aloft as an ideal totally beyond our imagination and our experience. This is not a picture of a perfect congregation, but it is a congregation made up of Christians.

Right up to the year 100 (if you take the book of Revelation as having been written then) John, writing under the inspiration of the Holy Spirit, directs the book of Revelation to individual churches. Hence, up to the end of the New Testament, individual churches existed and were important enough for letters to be addressed to them. The picture is clear. As Paul moves over the Roman Empire, as Aquila and Priscilla move over the Roman Empire, as other Christians move over the Roman Empire, individuals are saved and local congregations are organized. And this, I believe, is a pattern that holds for the church till Jesus comes.

The first biblical norm, then, is that there should be churches made up of Christians. Not to have such churches would be contrary to this norm.

Second, it seems clear that these congregations met together in a special way on the first day of the week. Though there are not many references, they do seem definite: Consider I Corinthians 16:2 and Acts 20:7. Each first day of the week they met as a statement that "He is risen, He is risen indeed!"

But let us notice that no specific time of the day is given as a norm. The day is set; the time of the day is left totally open.

local church polity

The letters of Paul and the book of Acts indicate something of the specific form these congregations took. We know, for example, that the churches had offices. Acts 14:23 reads, "And when they had ordained [or appointed] them elders in every church, and had prayed with fasting, they commended them to the Lord, on whom they believed." Scholars have discussed how these elders were chosen; I personally think that there is no clear indication. But there simply is no doubt of the fact that there were elders. The church did not sit there as a group of believers with no form. *The third norm, therefore, is that there are to be church officers (elders) who have responsibility for the local churches.* Missionaries on missionary journeys produced not only individual Christians, but also churches with officers.

elders and deacons

As one reads the New Testament, a rather detailed picture begins to emerge—the church begins to take on dimension and life. There is, for example, the remarkable passage (Acts 20:17-37) which describes Paul saying good-by to the church at Ephesus, a church he dearly loved and where he had spent so much time. He did not want to go to the city itself, where he knew he would be forced to stay longer, so he went to the seaport of Miletus, about 30 or 40 miles from Ephesus, and asked the elders to meet him there.

Paul then addressed this statement to them in the 28th verse: "Take heed therefore unto yourselves, and to all the flock, over the which the Holy Ghost hath made you overseers, to feed the church of God, which he hath purchased with his own blood." Notice how the elders are given a double charge. They are to watch out for those who will bring in false doctrine. They are called upon to exert discipline, but they are not only to be like a court, as if this is their only or their chief function. They are also to feed the flock. They have a responsibility to see that the church is not anemic. The elders are not to forget either side: Both are necessary. They must see that the Word of God is brought to the church so that, on the one hand, false doctrine and false life are kept out (or if they arise, that discipline is applied) but, on the other hand, that the church does not dry up like an old pea in a pod. They are to feed the church by the Word of God. This surely has the concept of teaching, but the use of the word *feed* carries more with it; it implies that the church is to live. The officers have a responsibility for maintaining real life in the church.

Paul implies in I Timothy 5:17 that there were two kinds of elders: "Let the elders that rule well be counted worthy of double honour, especially they who labour in the word and doctrine." Here, then, is an indication that in the early church some elders gave special attention to preaching and teaching. That is, there are elders who are especially committed to preaching and teaching the people, as it is expressed here, "labour in the word and in doctrine."

In addition to elders, there are also deacons. Acts 6:1-6 makes clear that they were the men who were to care for the distribution of gifts to meet the material need. *The fourth norm, then, is that there should be deacons responsible for the community of the church in the area of material things.* If the practice of community in the church were being taken as it should be, this would be no small task! They would indeed need to be men of the Spirit, as were the first deacons. Consider, for example, what this would mean when poorer blacks from the ghetto joined a more wealthy "middle-class" or "upper-class" congregation.

discipline

The fifth norm is that the church is to take discipline seriously. I Corinthians 5:1-5 is one example among many which calls for careful discipline based on the principle of the purity of the visible church in doctrine and in life. The New Testament stresses such purity, for the church is not to be just like an amoeba so that no one can tell the difference between the church and the world. There is to be a sharp edge. There is to be a distinction between one side and the other—between the world and the church, and between those who are in the church and those who are not.

Paul writes, "It is reported commonly that there is fornication among you, and such fornication as is not so much as named among the Gentiles, that one should have his father's wife. And ye are puffed up, and have not rather mourned, that he hath done this deed might be taken away from among you. For I verily, as absent in body, but present in spirit, have judged already, as though I were present, concerning him that hath so done this deed. In the name of our Lord Jesus Christ, when ye are gathered together, and my spirit, with the power of our Lord Jesus Christ, to deliver such an one unto Satan. . . ." The simple fact is that discipline in the church is important. For a church not to have discipline in life and doctrine means that it is not a New Testament church on the basis of the New Testament norms.

qualifications for office

The sixth norm is that there are specific qualifications for elders and deacons. Not only does the Bible set forth the offices of the church but it also describes the kind of men who should hold these offices. The qualifications for elders and deacons are given in two places—I Timothy 3:1-13 and Titus 1:5-9. These give what the elders and deacons should be like. The church has no right to diminish these standards for the officers of the church, nor does it have any right to elevate any others as though they are then equal to these which are commanded by God himself. These and only these stand as absolute.

In Titus 1:5 Paul writes, "For this cause left I thee in Crete, that thou shouldest set in order the things that are wanting [left undone], and ordain elders in every city, as I had appointed thee." So, although churches had been formed, the situation was still incomplete. The form was not yet full because elders had not yet been appointed or ordained. So Titus is to take care of what has been left undone; he is to bring this church up to the level of the form that the New Testament church should have.

the first church council

Form did not end with the local church. Acts 15 shows that these churches were not entirely separated one from the other. Representatives from individual churches at a time of real crisis met together in Jerusalem in what has often been called the Jerusalem Council. The issue was crucial: how a man is to be saved (Acts 15:1). It was a major doctrinal question bearing on the problem of the Judaizers who were saying that a man must be saved not only by faith in Christ but also by the addition of the Jewish ceremonial law: "Certain men which came down from Judaea taught the brethren, and said, Except ye be circumcised after the manner of Moses, ye cannot be saved." So they met together as office bearers (verse 6) in a formal way.

First of all, there was discussion (verses 7-12). The Authorized Version calls it "disputing," but this implies the wrong tone. There was much questioning, much discussion, but not what we would call disputing. Verse 7 reads, "And when there had been much questioning, Peter rose up, and said unto them, Men and brethren, ye know how that a good while ago God made choice among us. . . ." What follows is Peter's testimony in the situation. Afterwards, "all the multitude kept silence, and gave audience to Barnabas and Paul, declaring what miracles and wonders God had wrought among the Gentiles by them" (verse 12).

Hence, on the question of salvation there is discussion and testimony first by Peter and then by Barnabas and Paul. It would seem from the 13th verse that a kind of moderator is also present here: "And after they had held their peace, James answered, saying, Men and brethren, hearken unto me." There is very little detail as to the exact form here, but the general picture is clear. Somebody—James, the half brother of Christ—draws the discussion together and relates it to Scripture (verses 15-17)—the basis of the church's authority. Their solution was not merely something they generated out of themselves. It was rooted in Old Testament Scripture, in this case, Amos. James quotes, "After this I will return, and will build again the tabernacle of David, which is fallen down; and I will build again the ruins thereof, and I will set it up: that the residue of men might seek after the Lord, and all the Gentiles, upon whom my name is called, saith the Lord, who doeth all these things [or who maketh these things of old]." So here we find a meeting, a moderator, an appeal to Scripture and a conclusion. It does seem to me therefore that *the seventh norm is that there is a place for form on a wider basis than the local church.*

I would add as *the eighth biblical norm that the two sacraments of baptism and the Lord's Supper are to be practiced.*

form and freedom

Now it is important to realize two things here. First, these are the New Testament form commanded by God. These norms are not arbitrary—they are God's form for the institutional, organized church and they are to be present in the 20th century as well as any century. Second, there are vast areas which are left free. There is *form* and there is *freedom.*

Someone may feel that something else is clearly commanded beyond the eight norms I have given. Others may question whether one of these is really a norm. But do not let us get bogged down at this point. My primary point as we prepare for the end of the 20th century is, on the one hand, that there is a place for the institutional church and that it should maintain the form commanded by God, but, on the other hand, that this also leaves vast areas of freedom for change. It is my thesis that as we cannot bind men morally except with that which the Scripture clearly commands (beyond that we can only give advice), similarly, *anything the New Testament does not command in regard to church form is a freedom to be exercised under the leadership of the Holy Spirit for that particular time and place.*[1] In other words, the New Testament sets boundary conditions, but within these boundary conditions there is much freedom to meet the changes that arise both in different places and different times.

I am not saying that it is wrong to add others things as the Holy Spirit so leads, but I am saying that we should not fix these things forever—changing times may change the leading of the Holy Spirit in regard to these. And certainly the historic accidents of the past (which led to certain things being done) have no binding effect at all. It is parallel to the evangelical church being bound by middle-class mores and making them equal with God's absolutes. To do this is sin. Not being able, as times change, to change under the Holy Spirit is ugly. It is the same in regard to church polity and practice: In a rapidly changing age like ours, an age of total upheaval like ours, to make non-absolutes absolute guarantees both isolation and the death of the institutional, organized church.

---

[1] It seems clear to me that the opposite cannot be held, namely that only that which is commanded is allowed. If this were the case, then, for example, to have a church building would be wrong and so would having church bells or a pulpit, using books for singing, following any specific order of service, standing to sing, and many other like things. If consistently held in practice, I doubt if any church could function or worship.

5

the practice of community and freedom

L et us return for a moment to the concept of the orthodoxy of community in relationship to the task of the deacons who are responsible for the community of the church in the area of material things.

The Bible tells us the attitudes that should exist specifically in the churches of the Lord Jesus Christ and, I think we can say, in other Christian groups as well. Notice I Corinthians 16:1-2: "Now concerning the collection for the saints, as I have given order to the churches of Galatia, even so do ye. Upon the first day of the week let every one of you lay by him in store, as God hath prospered him, that there be no gatherings when I come." Here the tithe is not mentioned, but proportional giving is. They were meeting together on the first day of the week, as we meet on the first day of the week. And there was a call in the midst of the church to supply the needs of the saints.

Here is where I feel we, as evangelicals, have rather lost our way. We have made a complete distinction between our giving for missionary purposes and for the material needs of Christians. We have lost our way and ignored the tough stuff—the care of each other's material needs.

This is not by any means to minimize the giving for missions. Although Paul sometimes made tents, he also sometimes received gifts so that he did not need to make tents. True. But what I am pointing out is that there is no hard and sharp line in this giving. There is a strong emphasis on the fact that the local congregations within the proper polity had a huge sense of community—a sense of community which reached into all of life and all of life's needs, including the material needs.

how they love one another

The testimony has come down to us from the early churches—not in the Scripture but by an apparently accurate tradition—that in the Greek and Roman world the cry went out, "Behold, how they love one another." And I would suggest that this is precisely what we must be striving for. It is exactly parallel to marriage. According to the Scripture there is a form for sexual relationship. This form is not man-made, and it must not be set aside. This form is found in marriage.

But the difficulty within evangelical circles is that we often forget that within that marriage there is to be an interplay of personality which is beautiful within the proper form. There is both form and a freedom for reality of personal interplay within the form. The form is necessary. But we must understand that form is not all there is, or sexuality becomes frigid and dead. So if we have a totally faithful marriage that is also ugly, it is certainly not what it ought to be; it does not portray what God means marriage to be in the face of such a generation as ours. We can speak a great deal against sexual laxity in the whole area of sexual morality, but merely speaking of this is not enough. We must show to a world that is looking for beauty in the midst of 20th-century ugliness that in the proper form, marriage, there can be a freedom of personal interplay which is beautiful.

the practice of community

It is the same for the church. Let us hold until the time when Jesus comes the polity which the Bible gives us. And let us have community within the church that bears into all of life and all of life's needs—including the material needs. Recall the first positive characteristic required of an elder in Titus 1:8: that he is to be a man of hospitality. An elder is not only to measure up in some poor way to the negative stipulations. There is a positive: The elder's home is to be open to people. Here are the kinds of human relationships that are necessary to show community within our groups, to give what humanism longs for and cannot produce.

Humanism talks much of Man with a capital "M," but hardly anything of the individual man. It has produced a humanism out of the enlightenment that has ended in ugliness. We must exhibit community that truly is real and not just an inscription on a banner we carry on Saturday afternoon between four and five.

People are looking at us to see if, when we say we have truth, it is then possible for this truth not only to take men's souls to heaven, but to give all of life meaning in the present time, moment by moment. They are looking to us to produce something that will bring the world to a standstill—human beings treating human beings like human beings. The church should be able to do this because we know who we are and we know who they are—first, men made in the image of God, then brothers within the church and Christian community on the basis of the shed blood of the Lord Jesus Christ. The church will not stand in our generation, the church will not be a striking force in our generation unless it keeps a proper balance between form and freedom in regard to the polity of the church, unless it keeps the strength of the Christian dogmas and at the same time produces communities with beauty as well as truth.

All too often when people listen to the church, especially to the liberal church, they only hear God-words. And all too often they come to conclude when they listen to the evangelical and orthodox church that they also are hearing only God-words. And that should lead to our sorrow and our tears and our asking for forgiveness. When the Scripture talks about community and hospitality, it is not talking in vague generalities; it is talking about the stuff that counts and is open to observation. James writes, "If ye fulfil the royal law according to the Scripture," and here he goes back to Christ as giving the royal law, "Thou shalt love thy neighbor as thyself, ye do well" (James 2:8). And in verses 15 and 16, James under the leadership of the Holy Spirit puts teeth into the command: "If a brother or sister be naked, and destitute of daily food, and one of you say unto them, Depart in peace, be ye warmed and filled; notwithstanding ye give them not those things which are needful to the body; what doth it profit? Even so faith, if it hath not works, is dead, being alone."

There is no use saying you have community or love for each other if it does not get down into the tough stuff of life. It must, or we are producing ugliness in the name of truth. I am convinced that in the 20th century people all over the world will not listen if we have the right doctrine, the right polity, but are not exhibiting community.

This is not the world's call. It is God's call. Under the shed blood of the Lamb of God there is to be a substantial healing of everything that the Fall brought forth. It will not be perfect, but it must be substantial. And one of those things is the divisions between men. We must show by God's grace that in a substantial way these can be healed.

The book of Acts puts even more teeth in this: "Then the disciples, every man according to his ability, determined to send relief unto the brethren which dwelt in Judaea" (Acts 11:29). Here is something striking: The Greeks are sending money to the Jews. As the church at Antioch cut across the whole social spectrum, from Herod's foster brother down to the slave, the church and its community also cut across the difference between Jew and Gentile—not only in theory but in practice. When those in Antioch heard that the Jews had a material need in a different geographical location in Judaea, they gathered together their funds and sent them on a long journey in order to meet the material needs of their brothers.

Let me say it very strongly again: There is no use talking about love if it does not relate to the stuff of life in the area of material possessions and needs. If it does not mean a sharing of our material things for our brothers in Christ close at home and abroad, it means little or nothing.

At the very beginning of the New Testament church is the death of two people who lied to God at this particular point. "Neither was there any among them that lacked: for as many as were possessors of lands or houses sold them, and brought the prices of the things that were sold" (Acts 4:34). The communists say this is communism. It is not. Communism includes force. There is no force here. In Acts 5:4 Peter addresses Ananias: "Whiles it remained was it not thine own? and after it was sold, was it not in thine own power? why hast thou conceived this thing in thine heart? thou hast not lied unto men, but unto God." The church brought no force. The state was not involved. But there was a force stronger than that of any state in regard to the Christians' caring for each other's material needs, a force of love, a force of brotherhood and a force of community which covered all the facets of life.

freedom and form

Does the church have a future in our generation? Only if it shows not only the form of Scripture at the point of proper polity, but also the form of the Scripture at the point of proper community. If it does not show both together, we have missed the whole lot. One stands along with the other.

We call ourselves Bible-believing Christians. Some of us have stood together shoulder to shoulder since the early thirties in the battle for Bible-believing Christianity. That is beautiful. We must still stand regardless of the cost until Jesus comes. But let us understand that when I call myself a Bible-believing Christian, this cuts in two directions: It means that I speak when the Bible speaks, and I am silent when the Bible is silent.

Our forefathers understood this in the Westminster Assembly when they spoke of the fact that the church's authority was administrative and declarative. It meant that in the area of doctrine and the area of conduct, the church has a right to bind other people's conscience only where it could show that the principle was derived from an open exegesis of the Scripture.

We must speak where the Scripture has spoken. But let us notice that we must also respect the silences. Within every form, there is freedom. Whether one is painting a picture, or dealing with a sociological problem, or raising a child, it is the same. The formation of a school and the order in a school rests on the balance of form and freedom. I would suggest that where the Bible is silent, it indicates and reflects a freedom within the scriptural form.

God could have added one more chapter to the book of Acts and given us much more detail. He did not. We surely cannot say the Bible is mistaken. We must believe not only that what is said is—by God's will and inspiration—final, but also that where there is silence we are granted freedom under the leadership of the Holy Spirit.

If the church will allow freedom for changing situations, churches will be here until Jesus comes back. But let us not mistake historical accidents and what is sociologically comfortable out of our past for God's absolutes either in rules of personal dress or in the form that individual churches take in individual situations.

Can we not believe that the Holy Spirit will lead us in the area of silences? Is it not true that we Bible-believing Christians often cease being Bible-believing when we begin to teach that what is sociologically comfortable is equal with God's absolutes? I would suggest that many of us do it all the time.

Here is the feeling of death that so often people complain of. Here is the source of much of the confusion in our Christian schools and churches. The difference between God's absolutes and those things that are only a product of historic accidents is not understood.

I have an advantage because I work over many countries, and I see that godly people have been led by historic accidents into very different forms of the church. Different times are the same. There have been times when, in the early days, for example, the church met only in homes. Those of you who today meet in beautiful church buildings should thank God that he has given you a building bigger than a house in the midst of your needs. But do not confuse the building with an absolute. Do not confuse the church with a church building. It may burn to the ground. But destroying the building does not destroy the church.

There was a time when Priscilla and Aquila had a church in their home. Was that less a church? Of course not. What, then, does it indicate? It indicates that the Holy Spirit can lead at different times with freedom. Did he lead your group to build a building? I can well believe he did. Does it mean then that Aquila and Priscilla were wrong? No. Does it mean that Aquila and Priscilla were led of the Holy Spirit to have a church in their home? Yes. Does that mean you are wrong? No. So we have form and freedom.

The community we are called upon to make observable to the watching world is just as much an absolute form as the norms given concerning church polity. Community and polity stand together. But within this double form, there are freedoms in which the Holy Spirit may lead different people at different times, different congregations thereby meeting different needs.

ossified conservatism

The church has a place, but not if it ossifies. I think too often we are killing ourselves. We fail to distinguish the things that are open to change from those that are not. We must make ourselves available to the existential leading of the Holy Spirit. That is not the way we often think, especially those of us who are conservative. Sometimes people say we are conservative in our theology because we are conservative in everything. That is a jibe, but sometimes it is right.

Let me give two illustrations. The first is a group of German missionaries in South America. They have their own form. Their services must be in German because they have always been in German. And so they go to the Indians in South America and make them learn German so they can hear the gospel.

If that sounds too incredible—that surely your group is not so foolish—don't be too hasty. I know a church in the United States in which some of the people have a real burden for the blacks. It is a church that loves the Lord in its doctrine, and these people in it have achieved what I think is one of the outstanding breakthroughs in working with the blacks. One of the men in the church has felt this work is his special calling and has given much of his life to it. He gets up early every Sunday morning, wakes up the little children in the neighborhood and gets them out of bed. Because they have been up late at night, they must be awakened. He helps dress them and brings them to Sunday school. Here they are given graham crackers and milk, so the youngsters have something to eat.

But notice: These little children are not ready to get up for the morning church service at an early hour because in the ghetto they have been up half the night. So he suggested in this church—he was one of the elders—that they change the service to a later hour. And the roof fell in. A change was unthinkable. We may laugh or cry at the German missionaries, but this is surely as bad.

Many evangelicals and conservatives tend to be low church people. That is, very often they speak out against those who have any formalized form of liturgy. But in reality the low-church evangelical has his own form of liturgy which often is absolutely unchangeable. It is inconceivable to move the service from 10:00 to 10:45 or from morning to afternoon, or to change the order of the service, or to consider having the pastor stand in a privileged position only once on Sunday, rather than twice—to preach on Sunday morning, but answer questions Sunday night.

You have all sorts of possibilities. There should be different kinds of services at different places and different times. Many would be preferable to what most churches now have. May our churches be open to these possibilities.

an old-fashioned spiritual problem

Refusal to consider change under the direction of the Holy Spirit is a spiritual problem, not an intellectual problem. There is a bad concept of old-fashionedness and there is a good concept. The good concept is that some things never change because they are eternal truths. These we must hold to tenaciously and give up nothing of this kind of old-fashionedness. But there is a bad sense. I often ask young pastors and professors who are wrestling with these things a simple question: Can you really believe that the Holy Spirit is ever old-fashioned in the bad sense? The obvious answer is No. So if we as evangelicals become old-fashioned—not in the good sense, but the bad—we must understand the problem is not basically intellectual, but spiritual. It shows we have lost our way. We have lost contact with the leading of the Holy Spirit who is never old-fashioned in the bad sense.

There is a place for the church until Jesus comes. But there must be the balance of form and freedom in regard to the polity and the practicing community within that church. And there must be a freedom under the leadership of the Holy Spirit to change what needs to be changed, to meet the changing situation in the place and in the moment of that situation. Otherwise, I do not believe there is a place for the church as a living church. We will be ossified and we will shut Christ out of the church. His Lordship and the leadership of the Holy Spirit will become only words.

Let us be thankful there is a given form. Then let us be careful to make sure that we are not bound by unbiblical forms, by forms which we have become used to and which have no absolute place in the church of the Lord Jesus Christ. In regard to the polity and practice of the church, except for the clearly given biblical norms, every other detail is open to negotiation among God's people under the leadership of the Holy Spirit.

6

the threat of silence

believe the church today is in real danger. It is in for a rough day. We are facing present pressures and present and future manipulations which will be so overwhelming in the days to come that they will make the battles of the last 30 years look like kindergarten child's play.

The evangelical church seems to specialize in being behind. We now finally stand and talk about the pressures of the black-white crisis and the present urban problems. And, of course, these are real and a part of the whole, but the major problem we are going to face—as I see it, and I could be wrong and I hope I am—in the next 30 years is revolution with repression. Society is going to change. I believe that when my grandchildren grow to maturity, they will face a culture that has little similarity to ours. And the church today should be getting ready and talking about issues of tomorrow and not about issues of 20 and 30 years ago, because the church is going to be squeezed in a wringer. If we found it tough in these last few years, what are we going to do when we are faced with the real changes that are ahead?

We already are, of course, losing many of our young people, losing them on every side. It would be impossible to say how many have come to L'Abri from Christian backgrounds. And these young people have said, "You are our last hope." Why? Because they are smart enough to know that they have been given no answers, and they are opting out. They don't care about what will happen when they are 25. They don't even care if they are going to split their chromosomes by using drugs. The older generation hasn't given them anything to care about. They have simply been told to believe. Doctrines have been given them without relating them to the hard, hard problems which these young people are facing. This in itself should make us ask questions. Where are we going? And what is our problem?

what lies ahead

Whether we live in the United States, Britain, Canada, Holland or other "Reformation countries," it really does not matter. The historic Christian faith is in the minority. Most Christians, especially those of us who remember what the United States was like 45 or 50 years ago, go on as if we were in the majority, as though the status quo belongs to us. It does not.

One of the greatest injustices we do to our young people is to ask them to be conservative. Christianity today is not conservative, but revolutionary. To be conservative today is to miss the whole point, for conservatism means standing in the flow of the status quo, and the status quo no longer belongs to us. Today we are an absolute minority. If we want to be fair, we must teach the young to be revolutionaries, revolutionaries against the status quo.

Do you wonder why kids leave home? Youngsters come to L'Abri from the richest families in the world, from the greatest luxury. They come in their bare feet. They come in blue jeans. Why? Because they are sick of their parents making gods of affluence and thinking that one adds enough meaning to life merely by adding one more automobile to an already crowded garage. These young people are not wrong in this. They may have the wrong solution, but they are right in their diagnosis. Their parents, in the majority of what in 1970 is called the Silent Majority, may sound like Christians, but they have no base. They may say what we have heard in the past and they may say what Christians might say, but it is not the same. They are merely repeating from memory what is comfortable for the moment.

Here we are, then, the historic, Bible-believing Christian minority. What are the possibilities for the future? As the New Left and the anarchists come forward, more chaos will result. And as more and more chaos comes, the majority of the Silent Majority will increasingly tend to strike back. To do so, they will increasingly accept the Establishment elite.

What about the church in this situation? Certainly, at least at first, the Establishment elite will be less harsh on the church than the Left Wing elite if they should come into power. But that is a danger. The church will tend to make peace with the Establishment and identify itself with it. It will seem better at first, but not in the end. If the church is identified with the Establishment in the minds of young people, in the minds of those who will be coming forth to be the men and the women in the next 10 years and the next 20 years, I believe the church is finished.

In the United States many churches display the American flag. The Christian flag is usually put on one side and the American flag on the other. Does having the two flags in your church mean that Christianity and the American Establishment are equal? If it does, you are really in trouble. These are not two equal loyalties. The state is also under the norm of the Word of God. So if by having the American flag in your church you are indicating to your young people that there are two equal loyalties or two intertwined loyalties, you had better find some way out of it. The Establishment may easily become the church's enemy. Before the pressure comes, our young people (from kindergarten on), our older people and our officers must understand this well: There are not two equal loyalties—Caesar is second to God. It must be preached and taught in sermons, Sunday school classes and young people's groups.

It has always been so, but should certainly be so today. If a pastor stands in the pulpit and preaches this way, and the young people come in and hear him making plain that he is not confusing the two loyalties, then even if they differ on such a question as Vietnam, at least the pastor has maintained credibility with them. But the really important thing is not our credibility with other men, but our rightness with God. Equating of any other loyalty with our loyalty to God is sin. And we had better get our priorities straight now before the pressures in our society overwhelm both us and society as we have known it. If the pressures are great now there is every reason to be sure they will get greater.

pressures on society

In looking ahead into the next years at the end of this century, let us consider the special pressures on our society at this time, the pressures which open the way for a slide into accepting various forms of loss of liberty.

The first of these is the increasing loss of the Reformation memory as the years pass. This present generation has been raised by the first full post-Christian generation, and thus the memory is all but gone. In government and in morals the base is gone and the hedonistic, subjective whims of a 51% majority, or an elite, are all that is left. Only sociological averages and arbitrary judgments remain.

Because of the sweep of intellectual history—the philosophy and world views which cast away the revelational base, the modern, modern science that reduced man to a machine, the escape from reason that has led to the modern upstairs mysticism—the notion of a government and a law based on God's character and his revelation in Scripture is now no longer operative in political theory or in application. Even the very memory of it is all but gone.

Hence, society in the "Reformation countries" faces a major pressure—a pressure that strikes at its very roots. That which was its base is gone and the perspective with which everything else is viewed has shifted.

the loss of truth

A second, very closely related pressure is the fact that modern men no longer believe in truth. They no longer believe in antithesis. Modern man following Hegel believes only in dialectical synthesis. There is a thesis; it has an antithesis. Neither is true or false. "Truth" for today lies only in a synthesis. And even that synthesis is not true forever, for tomorrow there will arise another thesis different from today's and out of the combination of these will come "truth" for tomorrow. But in no case will any of these "truths" be absolute. *Truth* in the classical sense of that which accurately represents what is real for all time and all places does not exist—not even as an ideal.

This is just as true on our side of the Iron Curtain as it is on the other. If you could snap your fingers today—and I am not minimizing the danger of communism—if you could snap your fingers at this moment and there would be no communists left in the Western world, you would solve nothing. The real problem is that modern man, whether or not he is a communist, no longer believes in truth but only in Hegelian synthesis. Modern man thinks truth is unfindable. The generations that have preceded us may not have found truth, but they thought finding it was possible. They held it at least as an aspiration. Modern man no longer holds it as an aspiration.

Modern man no longer expects that truth exists even in the scientific world. All we are left with is statistical averages. Once I was speaking of science to a British university audience. Suddenly a young man in the scientific world stood up. "Sir," he said, "you don't realize how much the scientific enterprise is only the upper-middle class doing science as a form of gamesmanship." I am sure he is right. Often science is not engaged in the lofty objective of defining truth but in filling up the time with small details so that no great conclusions will have to be faced.

Furthermore, there are no philosophies in the traditional sense of philosophy. There are only anti-philosophies. Existentialism is an anti-philosophy because while it tries to deal with the really big questions, it does so apart from reason. Linguistic analysis, which dominates most of the universities today, does not even try to deal with the big questions. By definition they have shut themselves up and limited their work to the definition of language. They do not ask the big questions. Language leads to language.

This is the end of the Renaissance. The Enlightenment with all its humanistic pride has come to the place of despair.

Drugs, of course, add to the sense of a loss of truth as truth. And the destruction of normal syntax and normal language in the Theater of the Absurd, etc., is meant to hack away still further at any hope of truth.

Much of modern art, music and movies tends in the same direction. And most of all, the general acceptance of the absolute dichotomy of the upper and lower stories destroys truth as a unified concept and leaves modern man under the pressure of the relative.

the demise of aristocracy

A third pressure upon our society is that there is no natural leadership which can give direction to our culture. That is, there is no natural leadership class—no group in the United States or even Britain—who are respected and accepted as natural leaders, especially by the young. Of course, the situations in Britain and the United States are not exactly alike. The House of Lords, which used to give balance to the House of Commons, now could be removed and it would make practically no difference. The royal family likewise does little to maintain the government and cultural values—again, this is felt especially among the young. British aristocracy has become a kind of Wodehouse character to many people in England.

The simple fact is, however, that the same thing could be said about "the upper class" in the United States. No longer are there any such leaders who naturally command the respect and admiration of large bodies of American citizens, especially those under 30.

a sociological breakdown

A fourth pressure upon our society is the practical sociological breakdown. There are the hippies, of course, but it is not only the drop outs. Those who have a 9 a.m. to 5 p.m. mentality are everywhere today. Talk to any businessman, and he will tell you he can find few to take responsibility. Talk to the policeman on the beat, and he will tell you nobody will help him when somebody is in trouble.

Not long ago *Newsweek* carried a story of a policeman who was moonlighting by driving a taxi cab. Some people tried to hold him up. He had his revolver with him, so he got out and held them in the car. For over half an hour he pleaded with people to help him. Windows went up and then were slammed down. He stood there and he thought he could no longer hold out. Finally, a policeman on duty came along, and he was helped, but he had been caught in the midst of total sociological breakdown.

The worst case, of course, was the horrible thing that happened in New York a few years ago. A girl was gradually raped and stabbed to death while some 30 people who knew what was going on never even picked up a phone to call the police. They did not want to be involved.

The upshot is this: The whole of society treats men like machines because modern man has come to conclude that man is a machine. Those who think that our universities and our intellectuals are teaching that man is an animal are far, far behind. To modern man, man is only to be equated with clanking machinery. And as man sees man as a machine, he tends to treat men on the level of the sub-human.

Related to this is the whole effect of modern technology. The machine is given dominance over man. The machine is King. This would be serious and bring pressure under any circumstances, but when man does not know who he is and when he views other men as machinery, the pressure on society is overwhelming.

the population explosion and the ecological problem

A fifth great pressure that previous societies have never known is the population explosion and with it ecological destruction. These two could be discussed separately but they are closely related. The world is getting crowded. If you want to know what this means, think of yourself in your home. Then you move in twice as many people as you have now, then three times as many people. Pretty soon the temperature rises—the psychological temperature of men and women living in cramped quarters.

Do you ever have a feeling as you find yourself in a big city—so many people . . . so many people. As you drive down a crowded freeway—so many people . . . so many people. Think of the difference when man lived surrounded by acres and acres—and by quietness.

One would think that in the Alps where I live there would be peace, but everywhere you turn the mountains are being ripped up to make roads across them so that it is getting harder and harder to find a quiet place. We know the problem in the United States. So we make national parks, and pretty soon the national parks are destroyed because so many people come into them that the trails are covered with asphalt to keep them from being worn away, and they are no better than Broadway. The population explosion applies tremendous pressure.

Along with this goes total ecological destruction. We must not kid ourselves. We are in trouble. Not only Lake Erie is dead. Lake Geneva is sick. The ocean is dying. There is ecological pressure and the thinkers of this world are frightened about what is coming next. Read the papers carefully and you will see that, in ways open or not so open, the idea is being put forward that the only way to deal with the population explosion and the ecological problem is by an important curtailing of liberty.

the atomic bomb

Sixth, of course, is the pressure of the A-bomb or the H-bomb. For a certain kind of person this builds up a titanic pressure. Why? Because modern man has nobody in the universe but man. There is no God, there are no angels. And scientifically so far there is no proof that there is any other conscious life anywhere in the universe except on the earth. The only value that is left to a man like Bertrand Russell is the biological continuity of the human race. As Charlie Chaplin put it, "I feel lonely."

Modern man is lonely in a cosmic sense because as far as he is concerned, he is the only real conscious observer. He has been kicked up by chance and he is the only observer there is. If the hydrogen bombs drop in their total force and wipe out the human race, all that is left will be the universe, hard and cold, with nobody to look at it, nobody to observe it, nobody to see its beauty, nobody to see its order. There will be no one to see the blowing of a tree, hear the song of a bird, see the formation of a cloud or the rise of the sun. This is where modern man is living. And it is terrifying. What is the use? If the hydrogen bombs fall, the world is silent.

Think, if you will, for a moment what this would mean. Suppose you wrote the greatest sonnet that was ever written, and you put it on tape and hooked it up to a machine that has the highest amplification that any machine has ever been able to give. Suppose you hooked this up to solar batteries so that it would play for 1,000 years. Suddenly, then, suppose the hydrogen bomb dropped. There is no God, there are no angels, there is no conscious intelligent life anywhere else in the universe and all the galaxies that would be able to be conscious of the playing of the sonnet. What difference would it make if the sonnet played out in the unhearing, unheeding coldness of the galaxies even for 5,000 years? This is modern man's pressure.

the biological bomb

There is a seventh pressure which is the greatest yet. Especially in Europe scientists are wrestling with this. It is often called the biological bomb, a "bomb" much greater than the hydrogen bomb. I am not being spectacular: Within 20 years we will be able to make the kind of babies we want to make. The genetic engineers have made most of the basic breakthroughs on this.

Aldous Huxley's *Brave New World* was not a joke. As he described it, babies were grown in test tubes. They were bred in intellect and physical ability for the height of the labor the state wished them to perform. So if a man was needed for a certain manual job, he would be bred for that level, another man to another level and on up through the whole line. That was Huxley's vision thirty years ago. It is almost here today.

Modern man has no moral imperative for what he *should* do, and consequently he is left only with what he *can* do. And he is doing what he can do even though he stands in terror. And the biggest terror of all is: Who is going to make the babies? Who is going to know what kind of babies we need to make? Who is going to shape the human race?

It will not be just a matter of male and female, not merely a matter of preventing deformed babies. That is not where it ends. It is rather like Aldous Huxley and drugs. It is not that you give the drugs to the sick, but to the healthy. Here it is the same. Not just that you deal with a baby who may be born deformed. Now we are going to fool with the babies who are not deformed.

And with the development of the biological bomb, even today men are on the verge of being able to make new deadly viruses as super weapons, viruses for which there are no cures. Unlike the H-bomb, these will be easily made by any small nation.

where we stand

These, then, are some of the pressures on 20th-century society and the church. The collapse of the Reformational concept of government, the loss of truth, the demise of any aristocracy, the breakdown in personal responsibility, the population explosion and the ecological problem, the hydrogen bomb and the biological bomb—tremendous pressures these are! And these pressures open the way for the manipulators.

7

modern man the manipulator

t is obvious: The future is open to manipulation. Who will do the manipulating? Will it be the new elite on the side of an Establishment totalitarianism or the Left Wing elite? Whichever side wins—or whoever achieves political or cultural power in the future—will have at his disposal manipulations that no totalitarian ruler in the past has ever had. None of these are only future; they all exist today waiting to be used by the coming manipulators.

scientific manipulation

First of all, consider what Galbraith puts forward. He proposes that we turn everything over to the new philosopher kings of the academic and especially the scientific, state elite. But wait: Can we really trust the government of a scientist merely because he wears a white coat? Can we actually believe that such people will not manipulate just because they are scientists? One could give illustration after illustration where so-called scientific men simply no longer are really objective.

Recall that, as Alfred North Whitehead said, Christianity produced modern science because it gave a context in which the early scientists such as Galileo, Copernicus and Francis Bacon believed that the world could be understood by reason—it had been created by a reasonable God. Therefore, they were not surprised that man by his reason could find out the order of the universe. Modern man no longer has this assumption.

I am convinced that science as we have known it with a commitment to objectivity cannot continue now that this philosophy is gone. I work with many men in the scientific world, and many of them agree that objectivity is growing weaker. A clear illustration is Edmund Leach, a man who has given the Reith Lectures in England, a brilliant man, the leading anthropologist at the Cambridge University. Leach has said in *The New York Review of Books* (February 3, 1966) that in the past there were two theories of evolution. The most dominant theory that has held through the years is that the evolutionary process began in one place and therefore all races come from a common base. The second theory of evolution, which once was as strong as this although in the intervening years it has become much weaker and today is only a minor voice, is that evolution began at different points, widely separated not only in geographic location but in time. With this there is the concept that a race is higher if it has evolved longer.

Leach said in this article that the last time this second theory, this full theory of multiple evolution was put forward the man who stood against it was the president of Princeton University, a Christian. The reason he rejected it was theological.

Leach says that he does not stand against this other form of evolution for this reason, but because if one holds this view it promotes an attitude of racism, that one race is greater than another. Therefore, he chooses the other form of evolution.

Note well: This is a non-objective, sociological science. Conclusions are determined by the way a scientist *wants* the results to turn out sociologically. It is a science which will manipulate society by the manipulation of scientific "fact." I do not believe that man without absolutes, without the certainty that gave birth to modern science in the first place, will continue to maintain a high sense of objectivity. On one side, I think science will increasingly become only technology. On the other side, it will become sociological science and be a tool of manipulation in the hands of the manipulators.

Beware, therefore, of the movement to give the scientific community the right to rule. They are not neutral in the old concept of scientific objectivity. Objectivity is a myth that will not hold simply because these men have no basis for it. Keep in mind that to these men morals are only a set of averages. Here, then, is a present form of manipulation which we can expect to get greater as one or the other elite takes more power—and especially if the Establishment elite takes over.

manipulation of law

In a previous chapter we have already looked at the shift from the Reformation concept of law (which has a base to begin from in God's having spoken) to modern sociological law (in which the courts make law on the basis of what they conceive to be the immediate sociological good). In this view even the constitution and the previous body of law are viewed loosely as far as any constraint is concerned. Just as sociological science is a source of manipulation open to the manipulators, so sociological law gives either elite an endless range for manipulation.

manipulation of history

Another form of manipulation is the manipulation of history. In *Newsweek,* March 10, 1969, there was a little squib by Arnold Toynbee. He said that the races have always interbred in America and gave as proof of it that George Washington was out having sexual intercourse with a Negro slave in the slave quarters and he caught a cold, which was the cause of his death.

Even *Newsweek* felt it necessary to put a little note at the bottom of the page, saying that there is no authority for such a statement.

Is it a joke? No. People will be manipulated if they think you are talking history instead of mere subjective fantasy. There are dozens of such cases within the last couple of years.

History as history has always presented problems, but as the concept of the possibility of true truth has been lost, the erosion of the line between history and the fantasy the writer wishes to use as history for his own purposes is more and more successful as a tool of manipulation.

Take, for example, *Bonnie and Clyde*. Everybody thinks he knows the story of Bonnie and Clyde; everybody is sure he knows all about Bonnie and Clyde. The simple fact is that much in the movie is untrue. It was a sociological use of history brought down into films that had an impact on thousands and thousands of people who felt they were looking at truth in the form of history but were not. In fact, the film company was sued several million dollars by people who said that the truth had been distorted. The result was no less effective: The audience was manipulated.

Perhaps the clearest illustration is *Luther*, written by the English dramatist, John Osborne. This play made a great reputation for him, but it was a twisting of history, especially in the last lines. At the end of the play Martin Luther is challenged by Staupitz, the old man who supposedly had headed the monastery which Luther had left. Staupitz asks, "When you were before the Diet in Worms . . . why did you ask for that extra day to think over your reply?" Luther reflects and says, "I wasn't sure." Staupitz leaves, Luther takes his young son from his wife's arms and stands alone with the child softly talking: "We must go to bed, mustn't we? A little while, and you *shall* see me. Christ said that, my son. I hope that'll be the way of it again. I hope so. Let's just hope so, eh? Let's just hope so." The lights go out, and the play ends.

The *London Times* drama critic said, isn't it interesting that Osborne had to add that sentence in order to make it a modern play? Luther never would have said that. Luther's certainty based on the Bible is manipulated out of existence with one clever but false line that thousands took as history. Here is a distortion of fact, a destruction of Christian ideals and the Protestant base via contorted history.

The same thing can be said of Nat Turner. *The Confessions of Nat Turner,* written by William Styron, is supposedly the history of Nat Turner in his Negro revolution. But what most people do not realize is that all that we know about Nat Turner could be told in a very few pages. The rest of the book—including his sexual attraction to a white girl and the religious elements—is pure fabrication. Yet as a sociological tool of manipulation, the book is magnificent. People are open to manipulation if they think they are hearing history in a way that they never would be if they knew it was only fiction.

Michener's *Hawaii* is another perfect example. Here under the writing of what sounds like history a whole adverse view of Christianity is manipulated in the reader's mind. The same thing is true of Rolf Hochhuth's *Soldiers* in which Churchill is totally plowed. There is not an iota of evidence that Churchill had a Polish general killed. And yet Hochhuth by turning upon Churchill was able to manipulate with tremendous force against any concept of authority or power. The people who go to see this drama come away certain that Churchill was a knave and that you cannot trust anybody in authority.

manipulation in religion

Manipulation is on every side, and nowhere more so than in liberal theology and religion. Modern theology with its religious connotation words takes the words *Christ* or *God* or the other great Christian words and makes them a banner which has high motivation value but no content. The man who wishes to do the manipulation can simply grab the flag, march in the direction he wishes, and you are supposed to follow.

Perhaps the clearest illustration here is in situational ethics. The Cambridge morality following the Cambridge theology says it is Christ-like to sleep with a girl if she needs you. To call something Christ-like causes people to move in this direction without ever realizing that in so doing the sexual ethic of Jesus himself is being violated.

Salvador Dali's painting, not using words but symbols, does the same thing. Take his paintings of the crucifixion. Do not think his paintings painted after he finished being a surrealist and became a modern mystic present an historic event. Do not think that his *Lord's Supper*, now in the National Gallery, is talking about a space-time last supper. It is not. It is a mystical concept. Salvador Dali uses these symbols to say what Salvador Dali wishes to say. That is all.

The Beatles as they went through their cycle from rock, through drugs, to the psychedelic sound, then to Eastern religion did the same thing. They were manipulating on the basis of religious words.

I think, however, that the new theologians, both the Roman Catholic progressives and the Protestant theologians, are going to win in the use of contentless religious words. I would suggest that they stand in a stronger position than, say, the Beatles or Salvador Dali, for two great reasons. First, they have the continuity of religious organization. They control the machinery of almost every major denomination. Second, they use the same words that the ears of people are used to, and they do not bring in strange and exotic words such as the Beatles did.

I would not be at all surprised if in the future even communism will be manipulating its people on the basis of religious terms rather than atheism. I think there are signs of it in what the various theoreticians who are not Russian have been saying. Certainly, however, here in the West we are open to complete manipulation on the basis of contentless religious words. This is not theoretical: Remember that Julian Huxley, the atheist, has been suggesting this use of religion for years.

The ecological pressure opens the door to manipulation by religious terms in a different way. Many are saying that we must accept a concept of pantheism if the problem of ecology is to be met. Thus here pantheism is being suggested not as truth but as a form of manipulation of society.[1] It should be noted that this is not at odds with most liberal theology today, for most of it already has pantheistic tones.

manipulation in the theater and art

In the Theater of the Absurd, in Marcel Duchamp's environments and happenings, in much of television, in the cinema, in psychedelic sound, in light shows and in art, we are being removed from the control of our reason.

In art museums throughout the world the viewers are at the mercy of the artists. People, even children, who go through the art galleries are being manipulated whether they know it or not. No matter how long they contemplate, say, Duchamp's *The Bride Undressed by Her Bachelors Yet* or *Le passage de la vierge à la mariée* (The passage of the virgin to the married state), they may not understand the content of the painting. But the artist plays with the viewer as if he were putty. The young couple holding hands, looking at Duchamp's work will have a harder time saying No to their urges that evening. Reason is bypassed. Man is manipulated.

It should be noted most carefully that the giving up of the control of reason that is so universal today in the acceptance of the upper and lower

---

[1] For a book length treatment of this see *Pollution and the Death of Man: The Christian View of Ecology* (Wheaton: Tyndale House Publishers, 1970).

stories makes all these forms of manipulation that much more possible and complete.

manipulation in television

Television is perhaps an even worse offender. Malcolm Muggeridge has commented on this. He points out that people think they see reality when they see those television pictures, but what they do not realize is that they are looking at pure fantasy. They are looking at an edited situation that does not present what is but what the man at the console wants you to think is. You feel you know everything because you have actually seen the picture with your own eyes, but in every situation you have been given a completely edited version.

I learned this lesson the last time I was lecturing in St. Louis. I was speaking at a conference there and some people were kind and provided me with a room where I could get some rest. So my son Frankie and I went up to the room and he turned on the television set. As I sat there waiting for the next time I was going to lecture, I began to read in a paper about the war in Vietnam. On the television there was a war picture. Quite unconscious of what was happening, I read about the war in Vietnam and out of the corner of my eye watched the war picture. And all of a sudden it dawned on me that what I was looking at on the television screen which I knew with my mind was pure fantasy was more real in its impact than the war I was reading about in the paper where real people were dying. When what is shown on television is carefully edited, this force of the seen is then an absolute form of manipulation.

I have also been on the other end of this manipulation by editing when I have been on TV talk shows trying to make a point. Somebody at the controls knows that you are going to say something he does not like and so he switches the camera and the mike and you're dead. You sound like a fool no matter how right your answer is going to be. The television viewer says to himself, "Schaeffer is a fool"—and he may be, but this does not prove it. A simple fact: People think they are seeing reality when they sit in front of that crazy box, but they are being manipulated in subtle but strenuous ways.

Marshall McLuhan understands this. He has said some things that seem strange and farfetched, but what he is saying is serious indeed for the coming day. McLuhan divides all communication into hot and cool. Hot communication is any content that is filtered through the reason. Cool communication is that which brings a first-order reaction without filtering through the reason. He says, for example, that if a thief is going to rob a house, he puts meat down to distract the family dog. McLuhan says that that is the way we use things that seem to appeal to the reason on television. We distract the mind so we can get the result we want in a first-order experience.

Marshall McLuhan says, in fact, that democratic government is finished. What is going to be put in its place? Very soon, all of us will be living in the electronic village hooked up to a huge computer, and we will be able to know what everybody else in the world thinks. The majority opinion will become law in that hour. That concept is the way Sweden runs its sexual morality now. What the majority at that moment says is right is right. This is a Kinsey type of morality—sociological averages.

Closely related to this is the subliminal use of television and the cinema. You can flash something on any television or movie screen so fast that you never know you saw it and yet it affects you and you tend to do what you are told. This again is not theoretical: It has been perfectly proven. Once it was tested by flashing "Drink Coca-Cola, Drink Coca-Cola, Drink Coca-Cola" on a cinema screen. Nobody knew they had seen it and yet Coca-Cola was cleared out for blocks around after the cinema.

With Coca-Cola it may seem not to be serious, but with political manipulation it would be. By law no Western country may use this. But do we think that there are other countries under dictatorial rule that would not use it? Are we so naive? If a country really came down into the groove where I think our society is going, if one of these elites—the Establishment elite or the New Left elite—really took over power and in desperation it was this or nothing, are we so naive to think either of these elites would fail to use it? Let's not fool ourselves. No totalitarian government, including Hitler's and Stalin's, has ever had these forms of manipulation.

chemical and electrical manipulation

Arthur Koestler adds a further note. In *The Ghost in the Machine* he says that evolution is not yet complete. Not believing in the fall of man, he explains man's dilemma this way: Man has evolved with a lower and an upper brain that are not in harmony. What we must ask our scientists to do is to develop a super drug that will bring the two halves into proper relationship. Such a drug would make man passive and prevent his constant quarreling. How does Koestler propose that the drug be given to the population? Koestler has suggested that the way we may administer it is in the water supply.

Koestler is not alone in these suggestions of chemical or mechanical manipulation. *Newsweek* (December 1, 1969) says that by the 1990's drugs to blunt curiosity and initiative will be available for use. Either the Left Wing or Establishment elite would certainly use them. The *St. Louis Globe Democrat* (October 27, 1969) reported that Dr. Kermit Krantz, head of the Gynecology and Obstetrics Department of Kansas City University's medical school, urged putting "the pill" in all the world's water supplies if it would solve the problem of overpopulation. Whether "the pill" is ever so used or not, this form of manipulation is an acceptable concept in modern men's minds.

The *International Herald Tribune* (May 22, 1970) gave this report:

A scientist told a symposium here [Paris] about monkeys with tiny radios attached to their brains whose mischievous thoughts are "corrected" by computer before they put them into action.

The radio-controlled monkeys were reported by Spanish-born Dr. José M. R. Delgado, who now teaches at Yale University. He was reporting to a Unesco interdisciplinary meeting on human aggressiveness yesterday.

One group of chimpanzees, with tiny sensors in their brains attached to radio transmitter-receivers worn on a kind of helmet, has been placed on an artificial island at Holloman, New Mexico.

While they roam apparently free, their behavior is constantly monitored and modified by the computer.

Human patients suffering from psychomotor epilepsy have also had these instruments, called "stimoceivers," attached.

Dr. Delgado said that through such techniques the next five years will see "a revolution in the medical treatment of aggressive behavior as important as the appearance of antibiotics in the treatment of infectious diseases."

"If a person is behaving antisocially, there are chemical and electrical mechanisms that we can know and modify," he said.

This kind of manipulation is not future; it is present, and it has not only been used with monkeys but men. An elite can decide who has, and who has not, "aggressive behavior."

Furthermore, the computer itself is dangerous. The computer has entered into a new age: It can watch you. The great eye can be upon you—recording every single thing you do from your birth to your death. This too is not tomorrow, it is ready today. One computer expert on the West Coast, a man who has as many basic computer patents as anybody in the world, has become so disturbed by the big, all-recording banks of computers that he is spending the end of his life trying to make little inexpensive computers so that men can fight the big computers. The existence of the computer and the control it puts into the hands of those in power steps up the power of each of the forms of modern manipulation in the hands of the manipulators.

becoming aware

I hate being an alarmist, and I do not think I am. Anything I have said that is pure alarmism, I hope you will simply forget. But these things are something that the church must be aware of. Many young scientists come to L'Abri, and I half facetiously say to some of them, "Maybe the biggest contribution you can ever make to Christianity is to make something you can put on the spigot or the faucet that will strain out everything except water!"

The church is confronted with people who really believe that democracy is dead, who really believe that such an age is gone. I agree. Unless we can return to a Reformation base with real reformation and real revival, these two great elites, from the left and the Establishment, will exert such pressures upon society that life will be completely changed. These are the things the evangelical church should be getting prepared for.

evolutionary christianity

We are surrounded on every side with the loss of truth, with forms of manipulation that would have made Hitler chuckle, that would have caused the rulers of Assyria to laugh with glee. And we not only have the possibilities for these manipulations, but people are trained on the basis of the loss of truth and the loss of the control of reason to accept them.

Where are we? Exactly where Romans 1:21-22 says we are. Man has rebelled against God and God is letting man go on to the natural conclusion and man believes a lie. This is the end—the big lie. Our generation is more ready to believe the big lie than any in the history of Western Man.

This is not a day for a sleepy church—a church that is merely operating on the basis of memory and is afraid to be free where it needs to be free within the form of Scripture.

What then must we as Christians do? What do we need? The task of this final chapter is to answer those questions. First, I would direct attention to two general requirements. But our Christianity is nothing if not a practical, moment-by-moment affair. So I will end by giving some specific, practical suggestions. May the Holy Spirit lead you to see in them what is there for you.

hot christianity

First, for ourselves and for our spiritual children, we need a Christianity that is strong, one that is not just a memory. The games of yesterday are past. We are in a struggle that the church has never been in before.

Basically, let me paraphrase McLuhan and reverse him. He says in a day of cool communication, that is, in a day when you are manipulating people, if anybody wants to sell his product he must not use hot communication. In other words, when people have been trained to respond like a salivating dog to the ringing of a bell, you must not try to feed things through reason. It will not work.

I would reverse this. In a day of increasing cool communication, biblical Christianity must make very plain that it will deal only with hot communication. Biblical Christianity rests upon content, factual content. It does not cause people to react merely emotionally in a first-order experience.

Let me repeat from Chapter I, some evangelicals have their own form of Kierkegaardianism or cool communication. Patting people on the head, they say, "Don't ask questions, dear, just believe." This is an evangelical Kierkegaardianism.

It is even stronger than this. Much of our gospel, as we preach it, has little or no content. We sometimes fall into the trap of saying the same thing that the liberal says, but in our own evangelical jargon instead of his. Trying to be modern, we say something like this to young people, "Drop out. Take a trip with Jesus." What does that mean? Nothing. Gobble-dygook. It's a contentless statement without meaning.

We can see it in the theological area because many evangelicals today feel that it is safe now to praise Karl Barth, not understanding that Karl Barth was the one who really opened the door to the new theology and all that flowed from it. Many evangelicals are drifting in this direction by treating the early chapters of Genesis the way the new theology treats the whole Bible; namely, separating the Bible's statements about space-time history from "religious truth." If we are really going to preach into the 20th century, we must have the courage to understand this must not be done.

I would also remind you—as I have done in a previous book—of what J. S. Bezzant, an old-fashioned liberal, says in *Objections to Christian Beliefs*. Speaking of the neo-orthodox position, he writes, "When I am told that it is precisely its immunity from proof which secures the Christian proclamation from the charge of being mythological, I reply that immunity from proof can 'secure' nothing whatever except immunity from proof, and call nonsense by its name." A brilliant sentence. But we may do it under the name of evangelicalism if we do not make clear that we speak of true truth and if we let people in various areas and disciplines squeeze out from under the control of Scripture.

Every single preaching of the gospel must be related to strong content. We must not fall into the cheap solution of beginning to use these cool means of communication and cause people to seem to make professions of faith. If we fall into this kind of manipulation, we have cut Christianity down to the ground because we are only adding to the lack of reasonable control. We are throwing ourselves wide open to future problems. Christianity must fight for its life to insist that it deals with content.

The New Testament itself says that we must strain through the grid of reason everything that comes into our mind.

John says in I John, if a spirit, a prophet, knocks on your door tonight, what do you say to him? John says that you ask him an intellectual question—whether Christ has come in the flesh. This is a question of the reason and not of the emotions. It is one of the sharpest intellectual questions one could frame, because when you ask a prophet or spirit whether Christ has come in the flesh, you are asking him two things: whether Christ already has had an existence before the incarnation and whether the incarnation has taken place.

In other words, the Bible insists on the church of Jesus Christ dealing, in the words of McLuhan, in the area of hot communication.

This is no time for Christianity to allow itself to be infiltrated by relativistic thinking from either the secular or the theological side. It is a time for the church to insist as a true revolutionary force that there is a truth. It is possible to know that truth, not exhaustively but truly.

compassionate christianity

Second, our Christianity must become truly universal, relevant to all segments of society and all societies of the world.

Why are we in trouble with the blacks? Simple. When white evangelical Christians held the consensus, they did not have enough care and compassion for the blacks to "assimilate" them. Not that the white evangelical church should have made the blacks white or converted them to a mode of living dominated by "white" historical accidents. But that the Christians (regardless of their race or color) should have so loved the newcomers that they shared with them Christianity and all that flows from it, and especially made sure that the black pastors had as good a theological training as the white pastors.

What, then, would have resulted would not have been a violation or an elimination of a black man's blackness, but the black community today would be far different if white Christians had had proper compassion. And, furthermore, the white community today would be far different. It is our lack of compassion that has brought us to the place we are now.

Unfortunately, it is not just the blacks. It involves, for example, Jews as well. The rationalistic Jews of eastern Europe came into New York City by the thousands. What churches went out to reach them for Christ? Practically none.

We let them live first of all in Harlem—the early Harlem. There they were. We did not care. We took their labor. We left them alone. And now the rationalistic Jews and their children, with all the brilliance of the Jewish mind, are shaping our culture through the theater, through works of art, through writing in the newspapers and news magazines and elsewhere. That is where we are. We have an enormous guilt behind us for a lack of compassion, not just for the blacks, but for all the people we have ignored.

Think of black Harlem. You know what Harlem was called in days past—no longer of course? The poor man's Paris. Why? Because everybody thought he could go to Paris and could sleep with anybody he wanted to sleep with, do any creepy thing he wanted to do, if he paid enough money for it. In days gone by we made Harlem that. The white man made black Harlem his Paris for every kinky thing he wanted to do.

We have had an enormous lack of compassion. We have said that we believe that men are lost, but what evidence for this have we shown the world when it comes to the blacks and the Jews and others as well?

Now we are doing exactly the same thing with the new outsider—the young. What are we doing to assimilate this new radical element? Mighty little. We drive them away from us in school, in our churches and very often even in our families. If any of these young are different from us in the smallest detail, the most unimportant and unessential detail, we simply do not have love and compassion for them. I am talking about community. We fail to show any community at all if their life styles differ in any way from our own mentality.

The early Christian church cut across all lines which divided men—Jew and Greek, Greek and barbarian, male and female; from Herod's foster brother to the slave; from the naturally proud Gentiles in Macedonia who sent material help to the naturally proud Jews who called all Gentiles dogs, and yet who could not keep the good news to themselves but took it to the Gentiles in Antioch. The observable and practical love in our days certainly should also without reservation cut across all such lines as language, nationalities, national frontiers, younger or older, colors of skin, education and economic levels, accent, line of birth, the class system of our particular locality, dress, short and long hair among whites and African and non-African hairdos among blacks, the wearing of shoes and the non-wearing of shoes, cultural differentiations, and the more traditional and less traditional forms of worship.

I want to tell you it can work. In L'Abri—let me keep saying, it's far from perfect—what do we find? Many young people from evangelical circles come every year. They arrive and say we are from such and such a school, from an evangelical background, and you are our last hope. We have heard that there may be some answers here. What do they do? They try us out. They come to church in their bluejeans. They see if they are going to be accepted. The next Sunday they come in bare feet. And we have to pass the test. When we pass the test we can begin to talk, but we have to pass the test. This is community. This is compassion. This is the area where we have to function.

Is there any absolute reason to wear shoes, either to class or to church? I can't find it in the norms of the New Testament. Many a time our little chapel is jammed, and these students come and there they sit. I or the others who preach don't preach for twenty minutes; we preach for an hour and a quarter every Sunday morning. And these students come and sit. They sit with their bare feet, they sit in their bluejeans, and they sit in their weird clothes, and they learn that it doesn't matter to us.

In reality, therefore, I don't think we have to worry much about youth. What we have to worry about is the church. If the church is what it should be, young people will be there. But they will not just "be there"—they will be there with the blowing of horns and the clashing of high-sounding cymbals, and they will come dancing with flowers in their hair.

In the midst of its imperfections and the circle of its weaknesses, what is happening at L'Abri proves this to be the case. Even when the church is a little bit of what it should be, the young people will come. They will come in their own way, they will come from the ends of the earth when the church is in some poor fashion that which God meant it to be.

So much for general requirements. What about the specific tasks, the specific things we can do, by the power of the Holy Spirit, to make the church come alive for today—and tomorrow?

open your home for community

Don't start a big program. Don't suddenly think you can add to your church budget and begin. Start personally and start in your homes. I dare you. I dare you in the name of Jesus Christ. Do what I am going to suggest. Begin by opening your home for community.

I have seen white evangelicals sit and clap their heads off when black evangelicals get up to talk at conference times. How they clap! That's nice because six years ago the evangelicals would not have been clapping. But I want to ask you something if you are white. In the past year, how many blacks have you fed at your dinner table? How many blacks have felt at home in your home? And if you haven't had any blacks in your home, shut up about the blacks. On the basis of Scripture, open your home to the blacks, and if they invite you, go with joy into their homes. Have them feel at home in your home. Then you will be able to begin to talk with them and your church can jump across this division as it should, but not before. And if you are a black Christian, it all cuts equally the other way: How many whites have you invited to your home in the last year? How many have eaten at your table?

How many times in the past year have you risked having a drunk vomit on your carpeted floor? How in the world, then, can you talk about compassion and about community—about the church's job in the inner city?

L'Abri is costly. If you think what God has done here is easy, you don't understand. It's a costly business to have a sense of community. L'Abri cannot be explained merely by the clear doctrine that is preached; it cannot be explained by the fact that God has here been giving intellectual answers to intellectual questions. I think those two things are important, but L'Abri cannot be explained if you remove the third. And that is there has been *some* community here. And it has been costly.

In about the first three years of L'Abri all our wedding presents were wiped out. Our sheets were torn. Holes were burned in our rugs. Indeed once a whole curtain almost burned up from somebody smoking in our living room. Blacks came to our table. Orientals came to our table. Everybody came to our table. It couldn't happen any other way. Drugs came to our place. People vomited in our rooms, in the rooms of Chalet Les Mélèzes which was our home, and now in the rest of the chalets of L'Abri.

How many times has this happened to you? You see, you don't need a big program. You don't have to convince your session or board. All you have to do is open your home and begin. And there is no place in God's world where there are no people who will come and share a home as long as it is a real home.

the unantiseptic risk

How many times have you risked an unantiseptic situation by having a girl who might easily have a sexual disease sleep between your sheets? We have girls come to our homes who have three or four abortions by the time they are 17. Is it possible they have veneral disease? Of course. But they sleep between our sheets. How many times have you let this happen in your home? Don't you see this is where we must begin? This is what the love of God means. This is the admonition to the elder—that he must be given to hospitality. Are you an elder? Are you given to hospitality? If not, keep quiet. There is no use talking. But you can begin.

There is a different kind of unantiseptic situation. How many times have you had a drug-taker come into your home? Sure it is a danger to your family, and you must be careful. But have you ever risked it? If you don't risk it, what are you talking about the drug problem for if in the name of Christ you have not tried to help somebody in this horrible situation!

If you have never done any of these things or things of this nature, if you have been married for years and years and had a home (or even a room) and none of this has ever occurred, if you have been quiet especially as our culture is crumbling about us, if this is so—do you really believe that people are going to hell? And if you really believe that, how can you stand and say, "I have never paid the price to open my living place and do the things that I can do"?

I have a question in my mind about us as evangelicals. We fight the liberals when they say there is no hell. But do we really believe people are going to hell?

It's not only at L'Abri in the Alps where this has meaning. When I was a pastor, I knew what it meant to go down to the nightclubs at night and fish the drunks out at 3 or 4 o'clock in the morning and take them to their homes. Do you?

Back in the forties when my wife, Edith, had a black cleaning woman come in, she ate lunch with her every day. When they ate together, Edith put a candle in the middle of the table so the table setting would have beauty. Have you ever done that? This is the way community begins. There is no other way. Everything else is false if it is further away than this.

structure your church for community

I'll tell you another thing you can do. You can consider restructuring your regular church meetings. There is nothing in the Scripture that says you have to have a worship service at 10 o'clock Sunday morning. You could have it at any time—3 p.m., 10 p.m. or even 2 a.m. And think of the folly of some churches that dare not omit an "invitation" in the evening because that service must be "evangelistic." It is always evangelistic whether or not an unsaved person ever comes into that church. Try to stop it, and pretty soon people say you are not evangelistic because you are not going through a certain form. But you must try.

There is also nothing in the New Testament that says you have to have a prayer meeting on Wednesday night. Why, then, do you have such a prayer meeting? Because you have always had one on Wednesday night? But suppose nobody came on Wednesday night. Who says you can't have the prayer meeting on Sunday night? If you have young people or others who would come one time but not another, why not change your services?

We must have the courage to change all kinds of things in our services. Stay within the limits of the form of the New Testament, but count everything else free under the leadership of the Holy Spirit. Begin to talk to your boards, begin to talk to your session, have prayer meetings about what you can change in your service to make our churches living things in the generation which we are facing.

Furthermore, you can quit having so many meaningless meetings in your church. You can eliminate those that meant something yesterday but not today, and then officers and people can spend more time opening their homes to other people. Not just so everyone can sit with their feet up and watch the little black box for three more hours. But so that you can talk to your children about the things they need to know in such a day as ours, have some family life, read to your children. Then you can open your home to a wider community. There are dozens of meetings in almost every church that could just as well be scrapped—meetings that have nothing to do with the norms of Scripture and therefore are not sacred as such.

It isn't too hard to begin. Of course, as soon as you start, it will be difficult because often you will have to buck the evangelical establishment. But Christian kids who come to L'Abri speaking of the unreality they see among the evangelicals are not talking about this kind of home. If they saw their parents opening the door to the drug kids, to the kids with the long hair, if they saw them opening their home at expense to their furniture and rugs, if they were told to pray not merely for the lost out there somewhere, but for specific people whom they knew sitting at the table in their own home, the unreality could be gone.

Do you ever open your home to the crazy friends of your own children? When your kids come home and they have brought some crazy kook? And he wears long hair and strange clothes? And he comes with his transistor radio plugged into his ear? The kids that your own children bring, are they welcome? Ask them and you will get some honest answers. And we must cry.

If our children see us paying prices this way in our homes and then see it moving over and beginning in our churches, we can be sure that this sense of unreality that is such a blight, such a cancer in the evangelical church, will begin to dissipate.

The Bible says we are to give out cups of cold water. How many have we ever given out to the long-haired and barefooted boys? Don't try to get your church to begin if you haven't begun it for yourself.

Do you talk against the affluent society? That's another thing that we evangelicals are now good at. We are against the affluent society. How many times have you risked your share in that society, getting nicked and scratched in the name of Jesus Christ? How many times have you risked breaking the springs in your car crowding kids into it to take them somewhere? Don't talk about being against the affluent society unless you put that share of the affluent society which is your hoard on the line. And don't dare tell me that these things I'm saying are not a part of the teaching of the Word of God concerning rich and real community.

But Christian pastors come to me and say, "Don't you understand? If I begin this, I'm going to get kicked out of my church. If I bring blacks and the long-haired kids into my home, if I really get close to them and they begin to love me and trust me and then come to church, I may get kicked out." We send martyrs off to the end of the earth and say go ahead and die for Jesus Christ. Why not here at home?

A revolution is coming and is here. If we don't have the courage in Jesus Christ to take a chance of getting kicked out of our churches and being ostracized today, what are we going to do when the revolution comes in force? If we don't have the courage to open our homes and begin to enter these things into the churches, slowly begin to make the changes that can be brought within the forms of the polity of the New Testament, then don't be concerned about having courage when the pressure comes.

I think that if we fail to train our muscles in such little places, when the revolution comes—especially if it comes violently from the New Left—most of the evangelical church will just give way beneath it. We had better begin, because the revolution with all its manipulation is coming.

Pray that the Lord will send you the people of his choice. But don't pray that way unless, no matter who these people are across the whole board of 20th-century man, you are willing to take them into your home, have them at your table, introduce them to your family and let them sleep between your sheets.

It is a day of no small games. We need to teach a Christianity of content and purity of doctrine. And we need to practice that truth in our ecclesiastical affairs and in our religious cooperation if men, young or old, are to take our claim of truth seriously. We need to understand the difference between being a cobelligerent and an ally between the two rising elites which confront us, and not choose nor slip into having either one as an ally. We must have and practice an orthodoxy of community. And we must be free to change those things in our church polity and practice which need changing. We would have thought the Christians of North

Korea, for example, not only foolish, but resisting the wisdom of the Holy Spirit if, instead of going underground, they had maintained their old habits of time and place of meetings which would have made them vulnerable to those who desired to destroy them in the take-over of North Korea. Are we doing any better in the light of the overwhelming changes which have already come in our culture and society—to say nothing of being prepared for what is coming—as we stand facing the rising New Left and Establishment elites?

appendix I

adultery and apostasy
the bride and bridegroom theme

This study is one that I consider exceedingly important for our own generation: Adultery and Apostasy—The Bride and Bridegroom Theme. Ephesians 5:25b-32 reads: "Christ also loved the church, and gave himself for it; that he might sanctify and cleanse it with the washing of water by the word, that he might present it to himself a glorious church, not having spot, or wrinkle, or any such thing; but that it should be holy and without blemish. So ought men to love their wives as their own bodies. He that loveth his wife loveth himself. For no man ever yet hated his own flesh; but nourisheth and cherisheth it, even as the Lord the church: for we are members of his body, of his flesh, and of his bones. For this cause shall a man leave his father and mother, and shall be joined unto his wife, and they two shall be one flesh. This is a great mystery: but I speak concerning Christ and the church."

You have here a very remarkable and a very strong statement which Christ makes concerning the church as his bride. Notice, however, how God very carefully here intertwines this with the marriage relationship. The two ideas are so fused together that it is almost impossible in an exegetical study to divide them even with, as it were, an instrument as sharp as a surgeon's scalpel. Thus you have in Ephesians 5:21-25: "Submitting yourselves one to another in the fear of God. Wives, submit yourselves unto your own husbands, as unto the Lord. For the husband is the head of the wife, even as Christ is the head of the church: and he is the saviour of the body. Therefore as the church is subject unto Christ, so let the wives be to their own husbands in everything. Husbands, love your wives, even as Christ also loved the church, and gave himself for it." And verse 33: "Nevertheless let every one of you in particular so love his wife even as himself; and the wife see that she reverence her husband."

So there is here a very strong intertwining of teaching about the two relationships: the man-woman relationship, the Christ-Christian relationship and the Christ-church relationship.

When you examine the New Testament, you find that the brideship is thought of in two ways. In some places the emphasis is upon the fact that each Christian is, individually, the bride of Christ, and in other places it is the church as a unity that is the bride of Christ. But there is no contradiction in this; there is merely unity in the midst of diversity. The church is collectively the bride of Christ, and it is made up of individual Christians, each one of whom is the bride of Christ.

Paul says (verse 32) that he is speaking of a great mystery. What a tremendous mystery! The fact that Christ, the eternal second person of the Trinity, has become the divine bridegroom.

the biblical norm

Notice that this passage in Ephesians does not stand alone. In many places in the New Testament this same sort of illustration is used intertwiningly. In John 3:28-29, we find John the Baptizer introducing Christ under these terms: "Ye yourselves bear me witness, that I said, I am not the Christ, but that I am sent before him. He [that is, the Christ] that hath the bride is the bridegroom." In John's introduction of Christ to the Jewish people we find that he says, Here is the Lamb of God, and next, here is the one who is going to be baptized by the Holy Spirit and who is going to baptize by the Holy Spirit, and here is the bridegroom of the bride.

Romans 7:4 contains a very striking, almost overwhelming, use of this teaching: "Wherefore, my brethren, ye also are become dead to the law by the body of Christ" (and then comes a double "in order that") "*in order that* ye should be married to another, even to him who is raised from the dead." So we are dead to the law in order that we should be married to Christ. But that is not the end of it: "*in order that* we should bring forth fruit unto God." This overwhelming picture is that, as the bride puts herself in the bridegroom's arms on the wedding day and then daily, and as therefore children are born, so too the individual Christian is to put himself or herself in the bridegroom's arms, not only once for all in justification, but existentially, moment by moment, and then he will bear Christ's fruit out into the fallen, revolted, external world. In this relationship we are all female. This is the biblical picture, surely one that we would not dare use if God himself did not use it.

The Old Testament, like the New, emphasizes the bride and the bridegroom aspect. In the Old Testament it is God and his people: God is the husband of his people. In Jeremiah 3:14: "Turn, O backsliding children, saith the Lord; for I am married unto you." And, of course, there is no basic difference. The church continues. The church is new at Pentecost in one sense, yet in another sense it existed from the first man who was redeemed on the basis of Christ's coming work.

We have in II Corinthians 11:1-2: "Would to God ye could bear with me a little in my folly: and indeed bear with me. For I am jealous over you with godly jealousy: for I have espoused [engaged] you to one husband, that I may present you as a chaste virgin to Christ." And in the great culmination of Revelation 19:6-9 we have the picture of the church at the end of this era—when Christ has returned. And what is the great event? It is nothing less than the marriage supper of the Lamb: "And I heard as it were the voice of a great multitude, and as the voice of many waters, and as the voice of mighty thunderings, saying, Alleluia: for the Lord God omnipotent reigneth. Let us be glad and rejoice, and give honour to him: for the marriage of the Lamb is come, and his wife has made herself ready. And to her was granted that she should be arrayed in fine linen, clean and white: for the fine linen is the righteousness of saints. And he saith unto me, Write, Blessed are they which are called unto the marriage supper of the Lamb. And he saith unto me, These are the true sayings of God."

This theme which is seen throughout the Old and New Testaments culminates in this last great Lord's Supper where Christ himself now will serve his people. And there need be no hurry and there need be no rush, with millions and millions being served from the hands of the risen Lord. And they, being risen physically from the dead, will partake with their resurrected bodies. We look forward to this as we repeat the words of I Corinthians 11:26 each time in the Communion service: "For as often as ye eat this bread, and drink this cup, ye do shew the Lord's death till he come."

Thus we find that the man-woman relationship of marriage is stressed throughout the Scriptures as a picture, an illustration, a type, of the wonder of the relationship of the individual and Christ and the church and Christ. What a contrast this is to the Eastern thinking, when, for example, Shiva came out of his ice-filled cave in the Himalayas and saw a mortal woman and loved her. He put his arms around her, she disappeared and he became neuter. There is nothing like this in the Scriptures. When we accept Christ as our Savior we do not lose our personality. For all eternity our personality stands in oneness with Christ.

Just as there is a real oneness between the human bride and bridegroom who really love each other, and yet the two personalities are not confused, so in our oneness with Christ, Christ remains Christ and the bride remains the bride. This great understanding of the way Scripture parallels the human man-woman relationship and our union with Christ guides our thinking in two directions. First, it makes us understand the greatness and the wonder and the beauty of marriage and, second, it helps us to understand profoundly something of the relationship between God and his people and between Christ and his church. We understand in a real way something of this relationship as we understand in a real way something of the marriage relationship.

My personal opinion is that the marriage relationship is not just an illustration, but rather that in all things—including the marriage relationship—God's external creation speaks of himself. We properly reject pantheism, but the orthodox man is in danger of forgetting that God has created the objective world—all the parts of his external creation—not merely as an abstract apologetic, but so that it speaks of himself. The external, objective universe does speak of him. While God is not the world, the world is created by God to speak about God.

the Bible and sexual adultery

In our generation people are asking why promiscuous sexual relationships are wrong. I would say that there are three reasons. (There may well be more, but in this study I want to draw attention to these three.) The first one, of course, is simply because God says so. God is the creator and the judge of the universe; his character is the law of the universe, and when he tells us a thing is wrong, it *is* wrong—if we are going to have a God at all of the kind the Scripture portrays.

Second, however, we must never forget that God has made us in our relationships to really fulfill that which he made us to be, and therefore, too, a right sexual relationship is for our good as we are made. It is not to our real fulfillment to have promiscuous sexual relationships. This is not what God has made us for. Promiscuity tries to force something into a form which God never made it for, and in which it cannot be fulfilled.

The third is the reason we are dealing with most fully in this study: that we know promiscuous sexual relationships are wrong because they break the picture of what God means marriage, the relationship of man and woman, to be. Marriage is set forth to be the illustration of the relationship of God and his people, and of Christ and his church. It stands upon God's character, and God is eternally faithful to his people. And we who are Christians should live every day of our lives in glad recognition of the faithfulness of God to his people, a faithfulness resting upon his character and upon his covenants, his promises. The relationship of God with his people rests upon his character, and sexual relationship outside of marriage breaks this parallel which the Bible draws between marriage and the relationship of God with his people. Thus if we break God's illustration by such a relationship, it is a serious thing. Both in the Old and New Testaments the Bible speaks out strongly against all sexual promiscuity. Scripture does not deal with it lightly. Along with all other forms of wrong sexual relationships, the Bible condemns adultery. Adultery means the sexual unfaithfulness of a person who is married. The Bible never allows us to tone down the utter seriousness of adultery.

In Matthew 5:32, for example, Jesus says: "But I say unto you, That whosoever shall put away his wife, saving for the cause of fornication, causeth her to commit adultery: and whosoever shall marry her that is divorced committeth adultery." In the Jewish setting engagement was tantamount to marriage, and all forms of unfaithfulness are included here. What he is saying here is that unfaithfulness is so great a sin that the other person has a proper right to end the marriage upon the basis of adultery.

Then of course, in the Law in Exodus 20:14, one of the ten commandments says: "Thou shalt not commit adultery." The Old Testament was not only the religious book of the Jews, but also their book of basic civil law, and as such was related to the commands of God in the theocracy. In Leviticus 20:10 as well, God does not allow us to think that adultery is a small thing: "And the man that committeth adultery with another man's wife, even he that committeth adultery with his neighbour's wife, the adulterer and the adulteress shall surely be put to death." Furthermore Deuteronomy 22:22 reads: "If a man be found lying with a woman married to an husband [later there are other directions for the punishment of sexual intercourse with an unmarried woman], then they shall both of them die, both the man that lay with the woman, and the woman: so shalt thou put away evil from Israel."

The book of Proverbs over and over again warns against adultery and its serious consequences. In the book of Jeremiah God continues to speak concerning this. Look at the first part of verses 10 and 11 of Jeremiah 23: "For the land is full of adulterers" and then "For both prophet and priest are profane." The prophet and the priest are not free from adultery any more than the people are free from adultery. Jeremiah emphasizes the fact that indeed there is a great tragedy here: The people of God are given to adultery.

The book of Jeremiah came at a crucial time in the Jewish history, a time, we learn from Jeremiah 5:7-8, when they had an affluent economy. They were in a time of materialistic well-being, and at the same time they were under the judgment of God: "How shall I pardon thee for this? thy children have forsaken me, and sworn by them that are no gods: when I had fed them to the full [here is the affluent society], they then committed adultery, and assembled themselves by troops in the harlots' houses. They were as fed horses in the morning: every one neighed after his neighbour's wife." So they are fed, they are filled with affluency, their stomachs are full of food, they have time on their hands. In this situation, what do they turn to? They are like the horse that, well fed, stands and neighs on one side of the stall for the female that stands in heat on the other side of the stall. God uses overwhelmingly strong terms in discussing adultery.

The New Testament reveals exactly the same attitude. For example, in Galatians 5:19: "Now the works of the flesh are manifest, which are these; Adultery, fornication, uncleanness, lasciviousness, idolatry, witchcraft [etc.] ." This is not to say that sexual sin is worse than any other sin. Such a concept of sin is completely warped and twisted. If you compare this list of sins with the others in the New Testament, you will notice that sexual sin is not always, by any means, named first. The Holy Spirit very carefully breaks up the listing of the sins in the New Testament, thus indicating that, except for the great sin of turning from God, you must not put one above the other. Other sins are also sins, and so the lists sometimes mention them in one order, sometimes in another. But that is a different thing from forgetting that God very strongly condemns sexual sin. All sin is equally sin. Nevertheless, while this is true, God never allows us to tone down on the condemnation of sexual sin. Sexual sin shatters the illustration of God and his people, of Christ and his church.

the bride of Christ and spiritual adultery
But there is another level in our understanding of adultery. In II Corinthians 11:1-2, which we have looked at before, we read: "Would to God ye could bear with me a little in my folly: and indeed bear with me. For I am jealous over you with godly jealousy: for I have espoused you to one husband, that I may present you as a chaste virgin to Christ." Here is the first step: Men have become Christians and thus are the bride of Christ. Then Paul adds this in verse 3: "But I fear, lest by any means, as the serpent beguiled Eve through his subtlety, so your minds should be corrupted from the simplicity that is in Christ." Here is the second step: The bride of Christ can be led away and can become less than the bride should be. As there can be physical adultery, so too there can be unfaithfulness to the divine bridegroom—spiritual adultery.

No one is perfect. None of us is totally faithful to our divine bridegroom. We are all weak. Many times we are unfaithful in a positive or a negative way in our thoughts or our actions. But the Scripture makes a clear distinction between the imperfection of all Christians and the spiritual adultery which results when those who claim to be God's people stop listening to what God has said and turn to other gods. As far as the Bible is concerned, the latter is apostasy.

The Bible takes the great and tremendous sin of adultery and shows us how important it is. And then it takes apostasy (turning away from God), calls it spiritual adultery (turning away from the divine bridegroom) and says, This is even more important! But isn't that to be expected? If the Bible speaks out against breaking the illustration, shattering the symbol, how much more should we expect it to condemn the violation of the reality of which marriage is the symbol!

There is a stigma in the use of the term *adultery*, even in the world in the second half of the twentieth century. Even if there has been open and blatant adultery between a husband and wife, when they go to the law for a divorce, often the word is avoided and called something else—nice names, gentle names. The world still finds the term *adultery* to be something which it does not like, at which it winces. And it is the same with *apostasy*. Men like to tone down on these terms. They like to speak of these things in polite language. But God does not. The world still winces at the term *adultery*, even in the post-Christian second half of the twentieth century; but this is the term which God takes and applies as a strong phrase, like a knife, crying out to his people. We find he uses the term *adultery*, and parallel terms, over and over again, in regard to the people of God turning away from himself. In Exodus 34:12-15 he says: "Take heed to thyself, lest thou make a covenant with the inhabitants of the land whither thou goest, lest it be for a snare in the midst of thee: but ye shall destroy their altars, break their images, and cut down their groves: for thou shalt worship no other god: for the LORD, whose name is Jealous, is a jealous God: Lest thou make a covenant with the inhabitants of the land, and they go a whoring after their gods, and do sacrifice unto their gods, and one call thee, and thou eat of his sacrifice." When the people of God turned aside to these gods, the false gods round about, what does God call it? He says, Do you not understand what you are doing? You are going a whoring, you are caught in the midst of a spiritual adultery.

Leviticus 20:5-6 also uses the strongest terms: "Then I will set my face against that man, and against his family, and will cut him off, and all that go a whoring after him to commit whoredom with Molech [a false god I will be discussing later], from among their people." Notice here that God uses the same expression. For God's people to turn from God is spiritual adultery. Judges 2:17 says: "And yet they would not hearken unto their judges, but they went a whoring after other gods, and bowed themselves down unto them." The term "bowed themselves down unto them" is a sexual term used of a wife giving herself to her husband. And here God uses it with all this force when he says: Do you not see that you have acted like an adulterous woman bowing down in the sexual position before another man? In the book of Psalms (73:27) we read again: "For lo, they that are far from thee shall perish: thou hast destroyed all them that go a whoring from thee."

In Isaiah 1:21: "How is the faithful city become a harlot!" Who is this? This is Jerusalem, Jerusalem the golden. This is Jerusalem the city of God, Zion. What has she become? A prostitute. Why? Because she has turned from her rightful husband and become a street walker with false gods. And consider Jeremiah 3:1: "They say, If a man put away his wife, and she go from him, and become another man's, shall he return unto her again? shall not that land be greatly polluted? but thou hast played the harlot with many lovers; yet return again to me, saith the Lord." God is saying, My faithfulness, my faithfulness goes right on. What you are doing is wounding me. In regard to this passage, remember that the New Testament says the same thing: We can make the Holy Spirit sad (Eph. 4:30). He is a person, and when we turn away from him and teach and do those things which are contrary to the character of God as revealed in Scripture, we wound the Holy Spirit. He is sad. And the Old Testament says that when the people of God turn away from God, it is not nothing to God; it saddens the husband who is God.

The sixth verse of the same chapter continues: "The Lord said also unto me in the days of Josiah the King, Hast thou seen that which backsliding Israel hath done? she is gone up upon every high mountain and under every green tree, and there hath played the harlot." Here is a picture of the hills, of the trees, of the places where they worship. And Jeremiah says, These have become your lovers. The ninth verse says: "And it came to pass through the lightness of her whoredom, that she defiled the land, and committed adultery with stones and with stocks." He says, This is what you are worshipping instead of the living God. How does God describe it? He pictures it as a perverse adultery with these objects.

In Ezekiel 6:9 God is speaking, not Ezekiel. "I am broken with their whorish heart." God is saying about his people who have turned away into apostasy, "I am broken with their whorish heart, which has departed from me, and with their eyes, which go a whoring after their idols." Notice how God is concerned about his people. This is not a neutral thing, a matter of indifference, to God. God is not just a theological term, he is not a "philosophical other." He is a personal God and we should glory in the fact that he is a personal God. But we must understand that since he is a personal God, he can be grieved. When his people turn away from him, there is sadness indeed on the part of the omnipotent God.

Ezekiel 16:30-32 pounds on: "How weak is thine heart, saith the Lord God, seeing thou doest all these things, the work of an imperious whorish woman; in that thou buildest thine eminent place in the head of every way [this reference is to a brothel; God is saying, Your idols built on every street corner are like a brothel], and makest thine high place in every street; and hast not been as an harlot, in that thou scornest hire; but as a wife that committeth adultery, which taketh strangers instead of her husband!" This is pursued further in Ezekiel 23, where the whole chapter is given over to this concept. God says, There are two cities, Jerusalem in the south and Samaria in the north, and they have both committed spiritual adultery, and he describes it there in the strongest terms.

Let us move on to Hosea 4:12: "My people ask counsel at their stocks, and their staff declareth unto them: for the spirit of whoredoms hath caused them to err, and they have gone a whoring from under their God." Notice the last expression again, where the sexual picture is used so vividly by God. He says, This is what you have done, you have moved out and you have taken this position under another god, a god that is no god—a god that is nonsense, nothing more than a stick, nothing more than your own staff. You commit spiritual adultery with these things; this is who you are and what you are and where you are.

Notice also Hosea 4:13: "They sacrifice upon the tops of the mountains, and burn incense upon the hills, under oaks and poplars and elms, because the shadow thereof is good: therefore your daughters shall commit whoredom, and your spouses shall commit adultery." This points to another whole stream of biblical teaching that I will not discuss here except in connection with this one verse: The Old Testament says that if God's people turn away in spiritual adultery, it will not be long until the following generations are engaged in physical adultery, for the two things go hand in hand. And if any generation proves this, it is our generation. John Updike is right in his book *The Couples*. The whole novel is an illustration of the last pages: Here the church is burned down. In reality the church was "burned down" before the book began, and there was nothing left for Piet, the main character, except his promiscuous sexual life.

Our generation proves this with overflowing force. Let there be spiritual adultery and it will not be long until physical adultery sprouts like toad-stools in the land. In the 1930's liberalism took over almost all the church-es in the United States and in the 1960's our generation is sick with promiscuous sex. It is the same in Britain and other countries. These things are not unrelated: They are cause and effect.

Again in Hosea 9:1 we read: "Rejoice not, O Israel, for joy, as other people: for thou hast gone a whoring from thy God, thou hast loved a reward upon every cornfloor." Here again in Hosea 9 apostasy is spiritual adultery. Notice the form of speech God uses. A woman is out harvesting, and there is a freedom in the midst of the harvest. She takes a gift of money from some man to sleep with him on the cornfloor in the midst of the harvesting. This is what those who had been God's people had become: The wife of the living God is this in her apostasy.

You may say now, have we not read enough of these verses? We have not read the half of what you will find as you go through the Scriptures. God says, I do not want you to forget, I do not look upon spiritual adultery lightly.

I have deliberately chosen examples from all parts of the Old Testa-ment—sections from the Law, from different places in the historic books, from the books of poetry and from the prophets. The whole of the Old Testament speaks in the same terms and carries the same force, the same thrust, as it proceeds.

You may say, Is this not just an Old Testament view? The answer is, No, it is the way the New Testament speaks as well. Revelation 17:1-5 reads: "And there came one of the seven angels which had the seven vials, and talked with me, saying unto me, Come hither; I will shew unto thee the judgment of the great whore that sitteth upon many waters: with whom the kings of the earth have committed fornication, and the inhabi-tants of the earth have been made drunk with the wine of her fornication. So he carried me away in the spirit into the wilderness: and I saw a woman sit upon a scarlet coloured beast, full of names of blasphemy, having seven heads and ten horns. And the woman was arrayed in purple and scarlet colour, and decked with gold and precious stones and pearls, having a golden cup in her hand full of abominations and filthiness of her fornica-tion: And upon her forehead was a name written, MYSTERY, BABYLON THE GREAT, THE MOTHER OF HARLOTS AND ABOMINATIONS OF THE EARTH." And the Bible just slams the door. This language is defi-nitely not in the Old Testament alone. It is brought to its highest pitch in the New Testament when the apostate church of the last days, and the culture it produces, is described in these terms.

spiritual adultery today

Now, let us notice where we have come. When those who claim to be God's people turn aside from the word of God and from the Christ of history, this is far more heinous in the sight of God than the worst case of infidelity in marriage, for it destroys the reality, the great central bride-groom-bride relationship. I have taken care to emphasize that God does not minimize promiscuity in sexual relationships, but apostasy—spiritual adultery—is worse. And the modern liberal theologian is in that place. How do we look at it? I would suggest we must be careful to look at it no less clearly than God does. Consider the liberal theology of our day. It denies the personal *God who is there*. It denies the divine, historic Christ. It denies the Bible as God's verbalized Word. It denies God's way of salva-tion. The liberals elevate their own humanistic theories to a position above the Word of God, the revealed communication of God to men. They make gods which are no gods, but are merely the projection of their own minds.

As we describe their theories, we tend to dress them up in polite terms, in fine clothes, carefully weaving these clothes so as not to offend. We dress up our attitudes and statements in fine words in regard to the modern Roman Catholic Church, and we call it "the progressive theol-ogy." But it is not the progressive theology, it is a regressive theology, a humanism being spoken in classical Roman Catholic terms. In Protestant-ism, we call it "Liberalism," which is a strange word to apply to it, for it is only humanism spoken in classical Protestant terms.

Of course, we must treat men as human beings while having discourse with them, and that very much includes the liberal theologians. We must treat them as made in the image of God, even if they are actively in rebellion against God, and we must let them know that we love them as individuals. But this does not mean that we should forget that apostasy must be named as apostasy. Apostasy must be called what it is—a spiritual adultery. We must have politeness and struggle for human relationships with the liberal theologians with whom we discuss. But as to the system they teach, there is to be no toning down concerning what it is—spiritual adultery. As I said, in our generation we tend to tone down the word *adultery* in divorce cases, for we do not much like the word. Far more in the religious realm do we tone down the terms *spiritual adultery* and *apostasy*. But in doing this we are grievously wrong, because the Bible's perspective should be our own, and this is the way God speaks of it and

looks upon it, and so this is the way God's people are called to look upon
it.

This spiritual adultery is worse, much worse, than physical adultery.
But it is also much worse, let me say, than the Jews following their idols.
Oh, how God spoke out against the Jews following their idols! What strong
figures of speech he used in love in order to bring them to their senses. But
modern liberal theology is far worse than this, for it turns against greater
light, against greater blessing. Modern liberal theology is worse than following the Molech of old.

Do you know the facts concerning Molech? Molech, whose idol was in
the valley of Hinnon, was a heathen god whom the Jews were constantly
warned against following. What kind of a god was Molech? He was the god
of the sacrifice of new-born babies. This was the central act of his worship:
The first-born of every woman's body had to be sacrificed to Molech.
According to one tradition, there was an opening at the back of the brazen
idol, and after a fire was made within it, each parent had to come and with
his own hands place his first-born child in the white-hot, outstretched
hands of Molech. According to this tradition the parent was not allowed to
show emotion, and drums were beaten so that the baby's cries could not
be heard as the baby died in the hands of Molech. And there, I would say,
stand many in our day. Many of those who come to me, those with whom
I work, are the children destroyed by a worse than Molech. Men—men who
were supposedly the men of God—have stood by while their children were
eaten up by modern theology. And then we are told that there is supposed
to be no emotion shown.

Some of you who read this bear yourselves the marks of these things
from the background from which you come. All of us are marked by this
in some way, to some extent, because our Western post-Christian world
has been undercut by this liberal theology. Every scar this present generation has, every tear cried, every baby which some of you who read this
have willfully aborted, every drug trip you have taken, cannot be separated
from the fact that the church has turned away and become unfaithful.
This generation are the babies in the hands of Molech. And are we, as mere
dilettantes, supposed to stand by and hear their cries and cover them up
by beating loudly the drums of a profitless discussion? I tell you, No. We
are to weep and to act.

What is the liberal theology like? It can only be paralleled with what
God says in Proverbs 30:20 about the adulterous woman: "Such is the
way of an adulterous woman; she eateth, and wipeth her mouth, and saith,

I have done no wickedness." What a picture! Not everyone whose theology has been somewhat infiltrated by liberal theology should be likened to this, but the real liberal theologian (whether the old liberal-type theologian or the newer existential theologian) stands in this place. They say they have done no evil by their spiritual adultery, while not only the church but the whole post-Christian culture shows the results of their unfaithfulness.

There is no adulterous woman who has ever been so soiled as the liberal theology, which has had all the gifts of God and has turned away to a worship of something that is more destructive than Molech was to the babies whose parents were led astray from the living God to worship this idol. This is not a thing to take lightly. We must show love to the man with whom we discuss. Yes, and we fight for this at L'Abri. We must fight for the fact that he is not to be treated as less than a man. Nothing is more ugly than the orthodox man treating another man as less than a man and failing to show that he takes seriously Christ's teaching that all men are our neighbors. We do not discuss with the liberal only to win, but to help others, and to try to help him as well. But to treat lightly what liberal theology has done—not for a moment.

God's word for our generation

What does God say to our generation? Exactly the same thing that he said to Israel two thousand five hundred years ago when he said through Ezekiel: "I am broken with their whorish heart, which hath departed from me, and with their eyes, which go a whoring after their idols." I believe that this is how God looks at much of the modern church, and on our Western culture. I believe that this is how he looks on much of our cinema, much of our drama, much within our art museums. And above everything else this is the way he looks into the churches in which a gospel that is no gospel is being preached. God is saddened. Should *we* not be moved?

He is the same God, he is the living God, he is the unchanging God. He is the God who is there. And will he not do in the midst of this situation what he did in the midst of the Jewish situation in the time of Isaiah in the Northern Kingdom, and in the time of Jeremiah and Ezekiel and Daniel in the Southern Kingdom? Will he not judge our culture? Will he not call it adulterous? I tell you in the name of God he will judge our culture, and he *is* judging our culture.

Now, what should be our response? Listen to Jeremiah speak in 13:27: "Woe unto thee, O Jerusalem! Woe unto thee, O Jerusalem!" Indeed, as redeemed men we should know the joy of Christ, but as we look around us in much of the church and in our culture, can we fail to cry tears? Must we not also have this message? "Woe unto thee, O Jerusalem! Woe unto thee, O Jerusalem!" For like Jerusalem, much of the church has turned apostate. Within two or three generations in our Northern European countries we have turned aside. In Germany over a longer period, but in most of our countries so quickly have we turned aside: "Woe unto you, Woe unto you, O Jerusalem! Woe to you, O liberal church! Woe to you, O apostate Christendom!" We must say these words while we cry for the individual and while we never fail to treat him as a human being. We must not speak more lightly than Jeremiah. We must not be any less moved. Our response must not be merely a theoretical discussion of an intellectual nature. It must be the cry, "Woe, O liberal church! Woe, O apostate Christendom!"

It is not just a question of abstract theology that is involved, not just an academic difference. It is not that I should get my Ph.D. and go off and sit in some faculty and merely make polite academic conversation. It is the difference between loyalty to the living God and spiritual adultery—spiritual adultery against the Creator and the Judge of the universe. Spiritual adultery, mind you, against the only adequate bridegroom for Man—individual man and Mankind—the only adequate bridegroom for all men in all the world. Spiritual adultery against the only one who can fulfill the longing of the human heart. To turn away from the divine bridegroom is to turn to unfulfilledness. This is not only sin: It is destruction.

We have seen how desperately wrong and sinful physical adultery is, but notice that Jesus gives a priority. In Matthew 21:31 Jesus says to the religious leaders of his day: "Verily I say unto you, That the publicans and the harlots go into the kingdom of God before you." It is not that Jesus minimized the sexual sin, but here he tells the religious leaders of his day who have turned away from God that the harlots and those who collect taxes for the Romans will go into the kingdom of God before them. As these men walk through the streets and see such a woman walking down the way, they will not speak to her. They will not even look at her. They turn away from her. They show their disgust publicly. But Jesus is saying, Look at her! Don't you understand? She will get into the kingdom of God before you ever will. Both are sinful. But God himself in the words of Christ puts down a priority. Sexual sin is sinful, but spiritual adultery is overwhelmingly worse. God himself puts down a hierarchy in these things.

What is apostasy? It is spiritual adultery. No other words will do. This must be taken into account as we speak of *The Practice of Truth.* Do not be only academic when you speak concerning the new Molech. You yourself have the burn marks of the new Molech. Everyone in our culture—especially the university generation and younger—has them. Nobody escapes, even if he was raised in a Christian home and has been a Christian from the time he was young. There is not one of us in our culture who does not have some burn marks from the new Molech upon his skin—not one.

God's word for us

But for ourselves, we who by God's grace belong to the people of God, we who are Christ's, we who are God's, we who have been redeemed on the basis of the blood of the Lamb—let us understand that we are now called, on the basis of this study, to take one more most crucial step. We are *to act* as that which we are. Who are we? We are not just those going to heaven. But we are even now the wife of God. We are at this moment the bride of Christ. And what does our divine bridegroom want from us? He wants from us not only doctrinal faithfulness, but our love day by day. Such a study as this should not be ended by merely looking with strong perspective upon those who are unfaithful.

I must ask myself, "But what about you, Schaeffer?" And what about you, each one of you who knows the grace of God? What should be your attitude? Our attention must swing back now to ourselves. We have a crucial question to ask about ourselves.

We must ask, "Do I fight merely for doctrinal faithfulness?" This is like the wife who never sleeps with anybody else, but never shows love to her own husband. Is that a sufficient relationship in marriage? No, ten thousand times no. Yet if I am a Christian who speaks and acts for doctrinal faithfulness but do not show love to my divine bridegroom, I am in the same place as such a wife. What God wants from us is not only doctrinal faithfulness, but our love day by day. Not in theory, mind you, but in practice.

For those of us who are the children of God, there can only be one end to this study concerning adultery and apostasy. We must realize the seriousness of modern apostasy; we must urge each other not to have any part in modern apostasy. But at the same time we must realize that we must love our Savior and Lord. We must be the loving, true bride of the divine bridegroom in reality and in practice, day by day, in the midst of the spiritual adultery of our day. Our call is first to be the bride faithful, but that is not the total call. The call is not only to be the bride faithful, but to be the bride in love.

appendix II*

the mark of the christian

*This appendix has been published separately as *The Mark of the Christian* (Inter-Varsity Press, 1970).

Through the centuries men have displayed many different symbols to show that they are Christians. They have worn marks in the lapels of their coats, hung chains about their necks, even had special haircuts.

Of course, there is nothing wrong with any of this, if one feels it is his calling. But there is a much better sign—a mark that has not been thought up just as a matter of expediency for use on some special occasion or in some specific era. It is a universal mark that is to last through all the ages of the church till Jesus comes back.

What is this mark?

At the close of his ministry, Jesus looks forward to his death on the cross, the open tomb and the ascension. Knowing that he is about to leave, Jesus prepares his disciples for what is to come. It is here that he makes clear what will be the distinguishing mark of the Christian:

> Little children, yet a little while I am with you. Ye shall seek me; and as I said unto the Jews, Whither I go, ye cannot come; so now I say to you. A new commandment I give unto you, That ye love one another; as I have loved you, that ye also love one another. By this shall all men know that ye are my disciples, if ye have love one to another. (John 13:33-35)

This passage reveals the mark that Jesus gives to label a Christian not just in one era or in one locality but at all times and all places until Jesus returns.

Notice that what he says here is not a description of a fact. It is a command which includes a condition: "A new commandment I give unto you, That ye love one another; as I have loved you, that ye also love one another. By this shall all men know that ye are my disciples, *if* you have love one to another." An *if* is involved. If you obey, you will wear the badge Christ gave. But since this is a command, it can be violated.

The point is that it is possible to be a Christian without showing the mark, but if we expect non-Christians to know that we are Christians, we must show the mark.

men and brothers

The command at this point is to love our fellow Christians, our brothers. But, of course, we must strike a balance and not forget the other side of Jesus' teaching: We are to love our fellowmen, to love *all* men, in fact, as neighbors.

All men bear the image of God. They have value, not because they are redeemed, but because they are God's creation in God's image. Modern man, who has rejected this, has no clue as to who he is, and because of this he can find no real value for himself or for other men. Hence, he downgrades the value of other men and produces the horrible thing we face today—a sick culture in which men treat men as inhuman, as machines. As Christians, however, we know the value of men.

All men are our neighbors, and we are to love them as ourselves. We are to do this on the basis of creation, even if they are not redeemed, for all men have value because they are made in the image of God. Therefore they are to be loved even at great cost.

This is, of course, the whole point of Jesus' story of the good Samaritan: Because a man is a man, he is to be loved at all cost.

So, when Jesus gives the special command to love our Christian brothers, it does not negate the other command. The two are not antithetical. We are not to choose between loving all men as ourselves and loving the Christian in a special way. The two commands reinforce each other.

If Jesus has commanded so strongly that we love all men as our neighbors, then how important it is especially to love our fellow Christians. If we are told to love all men as our neighbors—as ourselves—then surely, when it comes to those with whom we have the special bonds as fellow Christians—having one Father through one Jesus Christ and being indwelt by one Spirit—we can understand how overwhelmingly important it is that all men be able to see an observable love for those with whom we have these special ties. Paul makes the double obligation clear in Galatians 6:10: "As we have therefore opportunity, let us do good unto all men, especially unto them who are of the household of faith." He does not negate the command to do good to all men. But it is still not meaningless to add, "especially unto them who are of the household of faith." This dual goal should be our Christian mentality, the set of our minds; we should be consciously thinking about it and what it means in our one-moment-at-a-time lives. It should be the attitude that governs our outward observable actions.

Very often the true Bible-believing Christian, in his emphasis on two humanities—one lost, one saved—one still standing in rebellion against God, the other having returned to God through Christ—has given a picture of exclusiveness which is ugly.

There are two humanities. That is true. Some men made in the image of God still stand in rebellion against him; some, by the grace of God, have cast themselves upon God's solution.

Nonetheless, there is in another very important sense only one humanity. All men derive from one origin. By creation all men bear the image of God. In this sense all men are of one flesh, one blood.

Hence, the exclusiveness of the two humanities is undergirded by the unity of all men. And Christians are not to love their believing brothers to the exclusion of their non-believing fellowmen. That is ugly. We are to have the example of the good Samaritan consciously in mind at all times.

a delicate balance

The first commandment is to love the Lord our God with all our heart, soul and mind. The second commandment bears the universal command to love men. Notice that the second commandment is not just to love Christians. It is far wider than this. We are to love our neighbor as ourselves.

I Thessalonians 3:12 carries the same double emphasis: "And the Lord make you to increase and abound in love one toward another, and toward all men, even as we do toward you." Here the order is reversed. First of all, we are to have love one toward another and then toward all men, but that does not change the double emphasis. Rather, it points up the delicate balance—a balance that is not in practice automatically maintained.

In I John 3:11 (written later than the gospel that bears his name) John says, "For this is the message that ye heard from the beginning, that we should love one another." Years after Christ's death, John, in writing the epistle, calls us back to Christ's original command in John 13. Speaking to the church, John in effect says, "Don't forget this . . . Don't forget this. This command was given to us by Christ while he was still on the earth. This is to be your mark."

for true christians only

If we look again at the command in John 13, we will notice some important things. First of all, this is a command to have a special love to all true Christians, all born-again Christians. From the scriptural viewpoint, not all who call themselves Christians are Christians, and that is especially true in our generation. The meaning of the word *Christian* has been reduced to practically nothing. Surely, there is no word that has been so devalued unless it is the word of God itself. Central to semantics is the idea that a word as a symbol has no meaning until content is put into it. This is quite correct. Because the word *Christian* as a symbol has been made to mean so little, it has come to mean everything and nothing.

Jesus, however, is talking about loving all true Christians. And this is a command that has two cutting edges, for it means that we must both distinguish true Christians from all pretenders and be sure that we leave no true Christians outside of our consideration. In other words, mere humanists and liberal theologians who continue to use the Christian label or mere church members whose Christian designation is only a formality are not to be accounted true.

But we must be careful of the opposite error. We must include *everyone* who stands in the historic-biblical faith whether or not he is a member of our own party or our own group.

But even if a man is not among the true Christians, we still have the responsibility to love him as our neighbor. So we cannot say, "Now here's somebody that, as far as I can tell, does not stand among the group of true Christians, and therefore I don't have to think of him any more; I can just slough him off." Not at all. He is covered by the second commandment.

the standard of quality

The second thing to notice in these verses in John 13 is the quality of the love that is to be our standard. We are to love all Christians "as I," Jesus says, "have loved you." Now think of both the quality and the quantity of Jesus' love toward us. Of course, he is infinite and we are finite; he is God, we are men. Since he is infinite, our love can never be like his, it can never be an infinite love.

Nevertheless, the love he exhibited then and exhibits now is to be our standard. We dare have no lesser standard. We are to love all true Christians as Christ has loved us.

Now immediately, when we say this, either of two things can happen. We can just say, "I see! I see!" and we can make a little flag and write on it, "We Love All Christians!" You can see us trudging along with little flags—all rolled up—"We Love All Christians!"—and at the appropriate moment, we take off all the rubber bands, unzip the cover, and put it up. We wave it as we carry it along—"We Love All Christians!" How ugly!

It can be either this exceedingly ugly thing, as ugly as anything anyone could imagine, or it can be something as profound as anyone could imagine. And if it is to be the latter, it will take a great deal of time, a great deal of conscious talking and writing about it, a great deal of thinking and praying about it on the part of the Bible-believing Christians.

The church is to be a loving church in a dying culture. How, then, is the dying culture going to consider us? Jesus says, "By this shall all men know that ye are my disciples, if ye have love one to another." In the midst of the world, in the midst of our present dying culture, Jesus is giving a right to the world. Upon his authority he gives the world the right to judge whether you and I are born-again Christians on the basis of our observable love toward all Christians.

That's pretty frightening. Jesus turns to the world and says, "I've something to say to you. On the basis of my authority, I give you a right: You may judge whether or not an individual is a Christian on the basis of the love he shows to all Christians." In other words, if people come up to us and cast in our teeth the judgment that we are not Christians because we have not shown love toward other Christians, we must understand that they are only exercising a prerogative which Jesus gave them.

And we must not get angry. If people say, "You don't love other Christians," we must go home, get down on our knees and ask God whether or not they are right. And if they are, then they have a right to have said what they said.

failure in love

We must be very careful at this point, however. We may be true Christians, really born-again Christians, and yet fail in our love toward other Christians. As a matter of fact, to be completely realistic, it is stronger than this. There will be times (and let us say it with tears), there will be times when we will fail in our love toward each other as Christians. In a fallen world, where there is no such thing as perfection until Jesus comes, we know this will be the case. And, of course, when we fail, we must ask God's forgiveness. But, Jesus is not here saying that our failure to love all Christians proves that we are not Christians.

Let each of us see this individually for ourselves. If I fail in my love toward Christians, it does not prove I am not a Christian. What Jesus is saying, however, is that, if I do not have the love I should have toward all other Christians, the world has the right to make the judgment that I am not a Christian.

This distinction is imperative. If we fail in our love toward all Christians, we must not tear our heart out as though it were proof that we are lost. No one except Christ himself has ever lived and not failed. If success in love toward our brothers in Christ were to be the standard of whether or not a man is a Christian, then there would be no Christians, because all men have failed. But Jesus gives the world a piece of litmus paper, a reasonable thermometer: There is a mark which, if the world does not see, allows them to conclude, "This man is not a Christian." Of course, the world may be making a wrong judgment because, if the man is truly a Christian, as far as the reality goes, they made a mistake.

It is true that a non-Christian often hides behind what he sees in Christians and then screams, "Hypocrites!" when in reality he is a sinner who will not face the claims of Christ. But that is not what Jesus is talking about here. Here Jesus is talking about our responsibility as individuals and as groups to so love all other true Christians that the world will have no valid reason for saying that we are not Christians.

the final apologetic

But there is something even more sober. And to understand it we must look at John 17:21, a verse out of the midst of Christ's high priestly prayer. Jesus prays, "That they all may be one; as thou, Father, art in me, and I in thee, that they also may be one in us; that the world may believe that thou hast sent me." In this, his high priestly prayer, Jesus is praying for the oneness of the church, the oneness that should be found specifically among true Christians. Jesus is not praying for a humanistic, romantic oneness among men in general. Verse 9 makes this clear: "I pray not for the world, but for them which thou hast given me; for they are thine." Jesus here makes a very careful distinction between those who have cast themselves upon him in faith and those who still stand in rebellion. Hence, in the 21st verse, when he prays for oneness, the "they" he is referring to are the true Christians.

Notice, however, that verse 21 says, "That they all may be one. . . ." The emphasis, interestingly enough, is exactly the same as in John 13—not on a part of true Christians, but on all Christians—not that those in certain parties in the church should be one, but that all born-again Christians should be one.

Now comes the sobering part. Jesus goes on in this 21st verse to say something that always causes me to cringe. If as Christians we do not cringe, it seems to me we are not very sensitive or very honest, because Jesus here gives us the final apologetic. What is the final apologetic? *"That they all may be one;* as thou, Father, art in me, and I in thee, that they also may be one in us: *that the world may believe that thou hast sent me."* This is the final apologetic.

In John 13 the point was that, if an individual Christian does not show love toward other true Christians, the world has a right to judge that he is not a Christian. Here Jesus is stating something else which is much more cutting, much more profound: We cannot expect the world to believe that the Father sent the Son, that Jesus' claims are true, and that Christianity is true, unless the world sees some reality of the oneness of true Christians.

Now that is frightening. Should we not feel some emotion at this point?

Look at it again. Jesus is not saying that Christians should judge each other (as to their being Christian or not) on this basis. Please notice this with tremendous care. The church is to judge whether a man is a Christian on the basis of his doctrine, the propositional content of his faith, and then his credible profession of faith. When a man comes before a local church that is doing its job, he will be quizzed on the content of what he believes. If, for example, a church is conducting a heresy trial (the New Testament indicates there are to be heresy trials in the church of Christ), the question of heresy will turn on the content of the man's doctrine. The church has a right to judge, in fact it is commanded to judge, a man on the content of what he believes and teaches.

But we cannot expect the world to judge that way, because the world cares nothing about doctrine. And that is especially true in the second half of the 20th century when, on the basis of their epistomology, men no longer believe even in the possibility of absolute truth. And if we are surrounded by a world which no longer believes in the concept of truth, certainly we cannot expect people to have any interest in whether a man's doctrine is correct or not.

But Jesus did give the mark that will arrest the attention of the world, even the attention of the modern man who says he is just a machine. Because every man is made in the image of God and has, therefore, aspirations for love, there is something that can be in every geographical climate—in every point of time—which cannot fail to arrest his attention.

What is it? The love that true Christians show for each other and not just for their own party.

honest answers, observable love
Of course as Christians we must not minimize the need to give honest answers to honest questions. We should have an intellectual apologetic. The Bible commands it and Christ and Paul exemplify it. In the synagogue, in the marketplace, in homes and in almost every conceivable kind of situation, Jesus and Paul discussed Christianity. It is likewise the Christian's task to be able to give an honest answer to an honest question and then to give it.

Yet, without true Christians loving one another, Christ says the world cannot be expected to listen, even when we give proper answers. Let us be careful, indeed, to spend a lifetime studying to give honest answers. For years the orthodox, evangelical church has done this very poorly. So it is well to spend time learning to answer the questions of men who are about us. But after we have done our best to communicate to a lost world, still we must never forget that the final apologetic which Jesus gives is the observable love of true Christians for true Christians.

While it is not the central consideration that I am dealing with at this time, yet the observable love and oneness among true Christians exhibited before the world must certainly cross all the lines which divide men. The New Testament says, "Neither Greek nor barbarian, neither Jew nor Gentile, neither male nor female."

In the church at Antioch the Christians included Jews and Gentiles and reached all the way from Herod's foster brother to the slaves; and the naturally proud Greek Christian Gentiles of Macedonia showed a practical concern for the material needs of the Christian Jews in Jerusalem. The observable and practical love among true Christians that the world has a right to be able to observe in our day certainly should cut without reservation across such lines as language, nationalities, national frontiers, younger and older, colors of skin, levels of education and economics, accent, line of birth, the class system in any particular locality, dress, short or long hair among whites and African and non-African hairdos among blacks, the wearing of shoes and the non-wearing of shoes, cultural differentiations and the more traditional and less traditional forms of worship.

If the world does not see this, it will not believe that Christ was sent by the Father. People will not believe only on the basis of the proper answers. The two should not be placed in antithesis. The world must have the proper answers to their honest questions, but at the same time, there must be a oneness in love between all true Christians. This is what is needed if men are to know that Jesus was sent by the Father and that Christianity is true.

false notions of unity

Let us be clear, however, about what this oneness is. We can start by eliminating some false notions. First, the oneness that Jesus is talking about is not just organizational oneness. In our generation we have a tremendous push for ecclesiastical oneness. It is in the air—like German measles in a time of epidemic—and it is all about us. Human beings can have all sorts of organizational unity but exhibit to the world no unity at all.

The classic example is the Roman Catholic Church down through the ages. The Roman Catholic Church has had a great external unity—probably the greatest outward organizational unity that has ever been seen in this world, but there have been at the same time titanic and hateful power struggles between the different orders within the one church. Today there is a still greater difference between the classical Roman Catholicism and progressive Roman Catholicism. The Roman Catholic Church still tries to stand in organizational oneness, but there is only organizational unity, for here are two completely different religions, two different concepts of God, two different concepts of truth.

And exactly the same thing is true in the Protestant ecumenical movement. There is an attempt to bring people together organizationally on the basis of Jesus' statement, but there is no real unity, because two completely different religions—biblical Christianity and a "Christianity" which is no Christianity whatsoever—are involved. It is perfectly possible to have organizational unity, to spend a whole lifetime of energy on it, and yet to come nowhere near the realm that Jesus is talking about in John 17.

I do not wish to disparage proper organizational unity on a proper doctrinal basis. But Jesus is here talking about something very different, for there can be a great organizational unity without any oneness at all—even in churches that have fought for purity.

I believe very strongly in the principle and practice of the purity of the visible church, but I have seen churches that have fought for purity and are merely hotbeds of ugliness. No longer is there any observable, loving, personal relationship even in their own midst, let alone with other true Christians.

There is a further reason why one cannot interpret this unity of which Christ speaks as organizational. *All* Christians—"That they all may be one"—are to be one. It is obvious that there can be no organizational unity which could include all born-again Christians everywhere in the world. It is just not possible. For example, there are true, born-again Christians who belong to no organization at all. And what one organization could include those true Christians standing isolated from the outside world by persecution? Obviously organizational unity is not the answer.

There is a second false notion of what this unity involves. This is the view that evangelical Christians have often tried to escape under. Too often the evangelical has said, "Well, of course Jesus is talking here about the mystical union of the invisible church." And then he lets it go at that and does not think about it any more—ever.

In theological terms there are, to be sure, a visible church and an invisible church. The invisible Church is the real Church—in a way, the only church that has a right to be spelled with a capital. Because it is made up of all those who have thrown themselves upon Christ as Savior, it is most important. It is Christ's Church. As soon as I become a Christian, as soon as I throw myself upon Christ, I become a member of this Church, and there is a mystical unity binding me to all other members. True. But this is not what Jesus is talking about in John 13 and John 17, for we cannot break up this unity no matter what we do. Thus, to relate Christ's words to the mystical unity of the invisible Church is to reduce Christ's words to a meaningless phrase.

Third, he is not talking about our positional unity in Christ. It is true that there is a positional unity in Christ—that as soon as we accept Christ as Savior we have one Lord, one baptism, one birth (the second birth), and we are clothed with Christ's righteousness. But that is not the point here.

Fourth, we have legal unity in Christ, but he is not talking about that. There is a beautiful and wonderful legal unity among all Christians. The Father (the judge of the universe) forensically declares, on the basis of the finished work of Christ in space, time and history, that the true moral guilt of those who cast themselves upon Christ is gone. In that fact we have a wonderful unity; but that is not what Jesus is talking about here.

It will not do for the evangelical to try to escape into the concept of the invisible Church and these other related unities. To relate these verses in John 13 and 17 merely to the existence of the invisible Church makes Jesus' statement a nonsense statement. We make a mockery of what Jesus is saying unless we understand that he is talking about something visible.

This is the whole point: The world is going to judge whether Jesus has been sent by the Father on the basis of something that is open to observation.

true oneness

In John 13 and 17, Jesus talks about a real seeable oneness, a practicing oneness, a practical oneness across all lines, among all true Christians.

The Christian really has a double task. He has to practice both God's holiness and God's love. The Christian is to exhibit that God exists as the infinite-personal God; and then he is to exhibit simultaneously God's character of holiness and love. Not his holiness without his love: That is only harshness. Not his love without his holiness: That is only compromise. Anything that an individual Christian or Christian group does that fails to show the simultaneous balance of the holiness of God and the love of God presents to a watching world not a demonstration of the God who exists but a caricature of the God who exists.

According to the Scripture and the teaching of Christ, the love that is shown is to be exceedingly strong. It is not just something you mention in words once in a while.

visible love

What, then, does this love mean? How can it be made visible?

First, it means a very simple thing: It means that when I have made a mistake and when I have failed to love my Christian brother, I go to him and say, "I'm sorry." That is first.

It may seem a letdown—that the first thing we speak of should be so simple! But if you think it is easy, you have never tried to practice it.

In our own groups, in our own close Christian communities, even in our families, when we have shown lack of love toward another, we as Christians do not just automatically go and say we are sorry. On even the very simplest level it is never very easy.

It may sound simplistic to start with saying we are sorry and asking forgiveness, but it is not. This is the way of renewed fellowship, whether it is between a husband and wife, a parent and child, within a Christian community, or between groups. When we have shown a lack of love toward the other, we are called by God to go and say, "I'm sorry. . . . I really am sorry."

If I am not willing to say, "I'm sorry," when I have wronged somebody else—especially when I have not loved him—I have not even started to think about the meaning of a Christian oneness which the world can see. The world has a right to question whether I am a Christian. And more than that, let me say it again, if I am not willing to do this very simple thing, the world has a right to question whether Jesus was sent from God and whether Christianity is true.

How well have we consciously practiced this? How often, in the power of the Holy Spirit, have we gone to Christians in our own group and said, "I'm sorry"? How much time have we spent reestablishing contact with those in other groups, saying to them, "I'm sorry for what I've done, what I've said, or what I've written"? How frequently has one *group* gone to another *group* with whom it differed and has said, "We're sorry"? It is so important that it is, for all practical purposes, a part of the preaching of the gospel itself. The observable practice of truth and the observable practice of love go hand in hand with the proclamation of the good news of Jesus Christ.

I have observed one thing *among true Christians* in their differences in many countries: What divides and severs true Christian groups and Christians—what leaves a bitterness that can last for 20, 30 or 40 years (or for 50 or 60 years in a son's memory)—is not the issue of doctrine or belief which caused the differences in the first place. Invariably it is lack of love—and the bitter things that are said by true Christians in the midst of differences. These stick in the mind like glue. And after time passes and the differences between the Christians or the groups appear less than they did, there are still those bitter, bitter things we said in the midst of what we thought was a good and sufficient objective discussion. It is these things—these unloving attitudes and words—that cause the stench that the world can smell in the church of Jesus Christ among those who are really true Christians.

If, when we feel we must disagree as true Christians, we could simply guard our tongues and speak in love, in five or ten years the bitterness could be gone. Instead of that, we leave scars—a curse for generations. Not just a curse in the church, but a curse in the world. Newspaper headlines bear it in our Christian press, and it boils over into the secular press at times—Christians saying such bitter things about other Christians.

The world looks, shrugs its shoulders and turns away. It has not seen even the beginning of a living church in the midst of a dying culture. It has not seen the beginning of what Jesus indicates is the final apologetic—observable oneness among true Christians who are truly brothers in Christ. Our sharp tongues, the lack of love between us—not the necessary statements of differences that may exist between true Christians—these are what properly trouble the world.

How different this is from the straightforward and direct command of Jesus Christ—to show an observable oneness which may be seen by a watching world!

forgiveness

But there is more to observable love than saying we are sorry. There must also be open forgiveness. And though it's hard to say, "I'm sorry," it's even harder to forgive. The Bible, however, makes plain that the world must observe a forgiving spirit in the midst of God's people.

In the Lord's prayer, Jesus himself teaches us to pray, "Forgive us our trespasses, as we forgive those who trespass against us." Now this prayer, we must say quickly, is not for salvation. It has nothing to do with being born again, for we are born again on the basis of the finished work of Christ plus nothing. But it does have to do with a Christian's existential, moment-by-moment experiential relationship to God. We need a once-for-all forgiveness at justification, and we need a moment-by-moment forgiveness for our sins on the basis of Christ's work in order to be in open fellowship with God. What the Lord has taught us to pray in the Lord's prayer should make a Christian very sober every day of his life: We are asking the Lord to open to us the experiential realities of fellowship with himself as we forgive others.

Some Christians say that the Lord's prayer is not for this present era, but most of us would say it is. And yet at the same time we hardly think once in a year about our lack of a forgiving heart in relationship to God's forgiving us. Many Christians rarely or never seem to connect their own lack of reality of fellowship with God with their lack of forgiveness to men, even though they may say the Lord's prayer in a formal way over and over in their weekly Sunday worship services.

We must all continually acknowledge that we do not practice the forgiving heart as we should. And yet the prayer is "Forgive us our debts, our trespasses, as we forgive our debtors." We are to have a forgiving spirit even before the other person expresses regret for his wrong. The Lord's prayer does not suggest that when the other man is sorry, then we are to show a oneness by having a forgiving spirit. Rather, we are called upon to have a forgiving spirit without the other man having made the first step. We may still say that he is wrong, but in the midst of saying that he is wrong, we must be forgiving.

We are to have this forgiving spirit not only toward Christians but toward all men. But surely if it is toward all men, it is important toward Christians.

Such a forgiving spirit registers an attitude of love toward others. But, even though one can call this an attitude, true forgiveness is observable. Believe me, you can look on a man's face and know where he is as far as forgiveness is concerned. And the world is called on to look upon us and see whether we have love across the groups, love across party lines. Do they observe that we say, "I'm sorry," and do they observe a forgiving heart? Let me repeat: Our love will not be perfect, but it must be substantial enough for the world to be able to observe or it does not fit into the structure of the verses in John 13 and 17. And if the world does not observe this among true Christians, the world has a right to make the two awful judgments which these verses indicate: That we are not Christians and that Christ was not sent by the Father.

when christians disagree

What happens, then, when we must differ with other brothers in Christ because of the need also to show forth God's holiness either in doctrine or in life? In the matter of life, Paul clearly shows us the balance in I and II Corinthians. The same thing applies in doctrine as well.

First, in I Corinthians 5:1-5 he scolds the Corinthian church for allowing a man in the midst of fornication to stay in the church without discipline. Because of the holiness of God, because of the need to exhibit this holiness to a watching world, and because such judgment on the basis of God's revealed law is right in God's sight, Paul scolds the church for not disciplining the man.

After they have disciplined him, Paul writes again to them in II Corinthians 2:6-8 and scolds them because they are not showing love toward him. These two things must stand together.

I am thankful that Paul writes this way in his first letter and his second, for here you see a passage of time. The Corinthians have taken his advice, they have disciplined the Christian, and now Paul writes to them, "You're disciplining him, but why don't you show your love toward him?" He could have gone on and quoted Jesus in saying, "Don't you realize that the surrounding pagans of Corinth have a right to say that Jesus was not sent by the Father because you are not showing love to this man that you properly disciplined?"

A very important question arises at this point: How can we exhibit the oneness Christ commands without sharing in the other man's mistakes? I would suggest a few ways by which we can practice and show this oneness even across the lines where we must differ.

regret

First, we should never come to such difference with true Christians without regret and without tears. Sounds simple, doesn't it? Believe me, evangelicals often have not shown it. We rush in, being very, very pleased, it would seem at times, to find other men's mistakes. We build ourselves up by tearing other men down. This can never show a real oneness among Christians.

There is only one kind of man who can fight the Lord's battles in anywhere near a proper way, and that is the man who by nature is unbelligerent. A belligerent man tends to do it because he is belligerent; at least it looks that way. The world must observe that, when we must differ with each other as true Christians, we do it not because we love the smell of blood, the smell of the arena, the smell of the bullfight, but because we must for God's sake. If there are tears when we must speak, then something beautiful can be observed.

Second, in proportion to the gravity of what is wrong between true Christians, it is important consciously to exhibit a seeable love to the world. Not all differences among Christians are equal. There are some that are very minor. Others are overwhelmingly important.

The more serious the wrongness is, the more important it is to exhibit the holiness of God, to speak out concerning what is wrong. At the same time, the more serious the differences become, the more important it becomes that we look to the Holy Spirit to enable us to show love to the true Christians with whom we must differ. If it is only a minor difference, showing love does not take much conscious consideration. But where the difference becomes really important, it becomes proportionately more important to speak for God's holiness. And it becomes increasingly important in that place to show the world that we still love each other.

Humanly we function in exactly the opposite direction: In the less important differences we show more love toward true Christians, but as the difference gets into more important areas, we tend to show less love. The reverse must be the case: As the differences among true Christians get greater, we must *consciously* love and show a love which has some manifestation the world may see.

So let us consider this: Is my difference with my brother in Christ really crucially important? If so, it is doubly important that I spend time upon my knees asking the Holy Spirit, asking Christ, to do his work through me and my group, that I and we might show love even in this larger difference that we have come to with a brother in Christ or with another group of true Christians.

costly love

Third, we must show a *practical* demonstration of love in the midst of the dilemma even when it is costly. The word *love* should not be just a banner. In other words, we must do whatever must be done, at whatever cost, to show this love. We must not say, "I love you," and then—bang, bang, bang!

So often people think that Christianity is only something soft, only a kind of gooey love that loves evil equally with good. This is not the biblical position. The holiness of God is to be exhibited simultaneously with love. We must be careful, therefore, not to say that what is wrong is right, whether it is in the area of doctrine or of life, in our own group or another. Anywhere what is wrong is wrong, and we have a responsibility in that situation to say that what is wrong is wrong. But the observable love must be there regardless of the cost.

The Bible does not make these things escapable. I Corinthians 6:1-7 reads,

Dare any of you, having a matter against another, go to law before the unjust [that is, the unsaved people], and not before the saints? Do ye not know that the saints shall judge the world? and if the world shall be judged by you, are ye unworthy to judge the smallest matters? Know ye not that we shall judge angels? how much more things that pertain to this life? If then ye have judgments of things pertaining to this life, set them to judge who are least esteemed in the church. I speak to your shame. Is it so, that there is not a wise man among you? no, not one that shall be able to judge between his brethren? But brother goeth to law with brother, and that before the unbelievers. Now therefore there is utterly a fault among you, because ye go to law one with another. *Why do ye not rather take wrong? Why do ye not rather suffer yourselves to be defrauded?*

What does this mean? The church is not to let pass what is wrong; but the Christian should suffer practical, monetary loss to show the oneness true Christians should have rather than to go to court against other true Christians, for this would destroy such an observable oneness before the watching world. This is costly love, but it is just such practicing love that can be seen.

Paul is talking about something which is observable, something that is very real: The Christian is to show such love in the midst of a necessary difference with his brother that he is willing to suffer loss—not just monetary loss (though most Christians seem to forget all love and oneness when money gets involved) but whatever loss is involved.

Whatever the specifics are, there is to be a practical demonstration of love appropriate to a particular place. The Bible is a strong and down-to-earth book.

A fourth way we can show and exhibit love without sharing in our brother's mistake is to approach the problem with a desire to solve it, rather than with a desire to win. We all love to win. In fact, there is nobody who loves to win more than the theologian. The history of theology is all too often a long exhibition of a desire to win.

But we should understand that what we are working for in the midst of our difference is a *solution*—a solution that will give God the glory, that will be true to the Bible, but will exhibit the love of God simultaneously with his holiness. What is our attitude as we sit down to talk to our brother or as group meets with group to discuss differences? A desire to come out on top? To play one-upmanship? If there is any desire for love whatsoever, every time we discuss a difference, we will desire a solution and not just that we can be proven right.

the difference of differences

A fifth way in which we can show a practicing, observable love to the world without sharing in our brother's mistake is to realize, to keep *consciously* before us and to help each other be aware, that it is easy to compromise and to call what is wrong right, but that it is equally easy to forget to exhibit our oneness in Christ. This attitude must be constantly and consciously developed—talked about and written about in and among our groups and among ourselves as individuals.

In fact, this must be talked about and written about *before* differences arise between true Christians. We have conferences about everything else. Who has ever heard of a conference to consider how true Christians can exhibit in practice a fidelity to the holiness of God and yet simultaneously exhibit in practice a fidelity to the love of God before a watching world? Who ever heard of sermons or writings which carefully present the simultaneous practice of two principles which at first seem to work against each other: (1) the principle of the practice of the purity of the visible church in regard to doctrine and life and (2) the principle of the practice of an observable love and oneness among *all* true Christians?

If there is no careful preaching and writing about these things, are we so foolish as to think that there will be anything beautiful in practice when differences between true Christians must honestly be faced?

Before a watching world an observable love in the midst of difference will show a difference between Christians' differences and other men's differences. The world may not understand what the Christians are disagreeing about, but they will very quickly understand the difference of our differences from the world's differences if they see us having our differences in an open and observable love on a practical level.

That *is* different. Can you see why Jesus said this was the thing that would arrest the attention of the world? You cannot expect the world to understand doctrinal differences, especially in our day when the existence of true truth and absolutes are considered unthinkable even as concepts.

We cannot expect the world to understand that on the basis of the holiness of God we are having a different kind of difference because we are dealing with God's absolutes. But when they see differences among true Christians who also show an observable unity, this will open the way for them to consider the truth of Christianity and Christ's claim that the Father did send the Son.

As a matter of fact, we have a greater possibility of showing what Jesus is speaking about here in the midst of our differences, than we do if we are not differing. Obviously we ought not to go out looking for differences among Christians: There are enough without looking for more. But even so it is in the midst of a difference that we have our golden opportunity. When everything is going well and we are all standing around in a nice little circle, there is not much to be seen by the world. But when we come to the place where there is a real difference and we exhibit uncompromised principles but at the same time observable love, then there is something that the world can see, something they can use to judge that these really are Christians, and that Jesus has indeed been sent by the Father.

love in practice
Let me give two beautiful examples of such observable love. One happened among the Brethren groups in Germany immediately after the last war.

In order to control the church, Hitler commanded the union of all religious groups in Germany, drawing them together by law. The Brethren divided over this issue. Half accepted Hitler's dictum and half refused. The ones who submitted, of course, had a much easier time, but gradually in this organizational oneness with the liberal groups their own doctrinal sharpness and spiritual life withered. On the other hand, the group that stayed out remained spiritually virile, but there was hardly a family in which someone did not die in a German concentration camp.

Now can you imagine the emotional tension? The war is over, and these Christian brothers face each other again. They had the same doctrine and they had worked together for more than a generation. Now what is going to happen? One man remembers that his father died in a concentration camp and knows that these people over here remained safe. But people on the other side have deep personal feelings as well.

Then gradually these brothers came to know that this situation just would not do. A time was appointed when the elders of the two groups could meet together in a certain quiet place. I asked the man who told me this, "What did you do?" And he said, "Well, I'll tell you what we did. We came together, and we set aside several days in which each man would search his own heart." Here was a real difference; the emotions were deeply, deeply stirred. "My father has gone to the concentration camp; my mother was dragged away." These things are not just little pebbles on the beach; they reach into the deep wellsprings of human emotions. But these people understood the command of Christ at this place, and for several days every man did nothing except search his own heart concerning his own failures and the commands of Christ. Then they met together.

I asked the man, "What happened then?"

And he said, "We just were one."

To my mind, this is exactly what Jesus speaks about. The Father has sent the Son!

divided but one

The principle we are talking about is universal, applicable in all times and places. Let me, then, give you a second illustration—a different practice of the same principle.

I have been waiting for years for a time when two groups of born-again Christians who for good reasons find it impossible to work together separate without saying bitter things against each other. I have longed for two groups who would continue to show a love to the watching world when they came to the place where organizational unity seemed no longer possible between them.

Theoretically, of course, every local church ought to be able to minister to the whole spectrum of society. But in practice we must acknowledge that in certain places it becomes very difficult. The needs of different segments of society are different.

Recently a problem of this nature arose in a church in a large city in the Midwest in the United States. A number of people attuned to the modern age were going to a certain church, but the pastor gradually concluded that he was not able to preach and minister to the two groups. Some men can, but he personally did not find it possible to minister to the whole spectrum of his congregation—the long-haired ones and the far-out people they brought, and, at the same time, the people of the surrounding neighborhood.

The example of observable love I am going to present now must not be taken as an "of course" situation in our day. In our generation the lack of love can easily cut both ways: A middle-class people can all too easily be snobbish and unloving against the long-haired Christians, and the long-haired Christians can be equally snobbish and unloving against the short-haired Christians.

After trying for a long time to work together, the elders met and decided that they would make two churches. They made it very plain that they were not dividing because their doctrine was different; they were dividing as a matter of practicability. One member of the old session went to the new group. They worked under the whole session to make an orderly transition. Now they have two churches and they are consciously practicing love toward each other.

Here is a lack of organizational unity that is a true love and unity which the world may observe. The Father has sent the Son!

I want to say with all my heart that as we struggle with the proper preaching of the gospel in the midst of the 20th century, the importance of observable love must come into our message. We must not forget the final apologetic. The world has a right to look upon us as we, as true Christians, come to practical differences and it should be able to observe that we do love each other. Our love must have a form that the world may observe; it must be seeable.

the one true mark

Let us look again at the biblical texts which so clearly indicate the mark of the Christian:

A new commandment I give unto you, That ye love one another; as I have loved you, that ye also love one another. By this shall all men know that ye are my disciples, if ye have love one to another. (John 13:34-35)

That they all may be one; as thou, Father, art in me, and I in thee, that they also may be one in us: that the world may believe that thou hast sent me. (John 17:21)

What then shall we conclude but that as the Samaritan loved the wounded man, we as Christians are called upon to love *all* men as neighbors, loving them as ourselves. Second, that we are to love all true Christian brothers in a way that the world may observe. This means showing love to our brothers in the midst of our differences—great or small—loving our brothers when it costs us something, loving them even under times of tremendous emotional tension, loving them in a way the world can see. In short, we are to practice and exhibit the holiness of God and the love of God, for without this we grieve the Holy Spirit.

Love—and the unity it attests to—is the mark Christ gave Christians to *wear* before the world. Only with this mark may the world know that Christians are indeed Christians and that Jesus was sent by the Father.